straight talk
about homosexuality

The Other Side
of Tolerance

Richard Cohen, M.A.

PATH Press

PATH Press
P.O. Box 2315
Bowie, MD 20718
Tel. 301-805-5155
Fax 301-805-0182
www.pathinfo.org

Printed in the United States of America

Contents

Dedication

I dedicate this book to all who pursue the truth in love.

It is my fervent hope that the information contained
on the following pages will help to set the record straight,
heal the brokenhearted, and set the captives free.

Acknowledgments

Thanks to my beautiful and faithful wife Jae Sook. I love and appreciate you, forever.

Thanks to our three incredible children Jarish, Jessica, and Alfred. You are all magnificent. I love you with all my heart.

Thanks to Carlos and Minty for having the vision to support this work and bring more truth and light into the world. You and your family are my heroes.

Thanks to my beautiful and loving sister, Lyd. I appreciate you and Lloyd. You were always there for me, especially during the most difficult years.

Thanks to Christopher Doyle, Arthur Goldberg, Jessica Cohen, Hilde Wiemann, and Desiree Carlson for your invaluable suggestions to improve this text. You are all beautiful human beings.

Introduction

Truth without love is blind. Love without truth is deadly.

Richard Cohen

t is time to bring understanding to the confusing issue of homosexuality. It is time to set the record straight and answer key questions, separating fact from fiction. Are people born with same-sex attraction (SSA)? Did God make them that way? Did they choose to have SSA? Does God really love those who experience homosexual feelings? How do we respond to SSA family members, friends, and co-workers?

Straight Talk About Homosexuality will illuminate basic truths about homosexuality and present simple suggestions that you may incorporate into everyday life. It will offer rational answers about this very emotionally charged and volatile issue. *Through understanding and compassion, we can resolve in a loving way the controversies and confusion surrounding homosexuality.*

Why should *you* read a book about homosexuality? Why should *you* care? For just a moment, let me suggest to you why:

If you are a parent, you might have a child who one day proclaims, "I'm gay." If you are a son or daughter, you might have a mom who comes out and announces, "I'm a lesbian." If you are a brother or sister, cousin or relative, you might have a family member who says, "I'm gay." It's even possible that you might marry someone who one day reveals to you, after many years of marriage, "I think I'm gay."

Generally we need a personal connection to an issue to make it real. For instance, I came to recognize the pain and suffering of prison inmates after a close friend of mine was incarcerated. I visited him regularly and we wrote often. Hearing about his pain moved my heart and increased my awareness about the difficulties experienced by those who live in a world hidden behind bars. Previous to this, I never had inkling what it was like to live in prison. Visiting him, writing to him, and seeing his hurt and that of his family made this issue come alive in my life. Now I personally care about how the penal system treats those who are incarcerated.

I am a man who can give *you* an insider's look into homosexuality. I lived a homosexual life and had a same-sex partner for three years. Today I am a heterosexual man; I have been married to my wife for over 35 years and we have three incredible children. I have also served as a psychotherapist for 27 years, and in the process, I have helped hundreds of men and women who experience unwanted same-sex attraction (SSA) fulfill their heterosexual dreams. Through healing seminars, teleconferencing classes, and resource materials, I have literally helped thousands worldwide find freedom from unwanted homosexual feelings. I have also helped thousands of parents reconcile with their SSA loved ones, and in many cases, they were able to assist their children in coming out of homosexuality, even though they initially had no desire for change. This was done by setting love in order and demonstrating unconditional regard for their children.

Imagine what it would feel like if *you* were in school, sitting at the lunch room table, and no one wanted to sit next to *you*, no one wanted *you* at their table—"faggot," "queer," "sissy," "dyke"—just some of the names you might be called. No one wants to be seen with you…

Imagine *you* are at church or synagogue, and the pastor or rabbi is preaching, "Homosexuality is a sin!" All the while, unbeknownst to your family and friends, *you* experience same-sex attractions. What's more, you never, ever wanted those desires in the first place. What do you do?

Imagine *you* prayed month after month, year after year, "God, please take these homosexual desires away! I don't want them. I never asked for them. Please dear God, if you care about me at all, take them away. I beg you." But the desires continue no matter how many tears you've shed, and no matter how much you prayed, you still experience same-sex attraction (SSA), and that's that. What do you do?

These are just some of the experiences same-sex-attracted men and women around the world go through on a daily basis, along with the slings and arrows of outrageous discrimination and persecution for feelings they never chose to have. What would *you* do if it were *your* son or daughter, brother or sister, family member or friend who experienced SSA? Today, almost every person knows someone who experiences same-sex attraction.

Here are some issues I hope to share with you in this book:

- How the "gay" phenomena has become so pervasive in our world today
- The basic causes behind homosexual feelings in men and women
- Clues why five celebrities experience SSA
- How the use of words can promote healing in the world
- How to love SSA men and women the right way

It is quite possible that you have been indoctrinated into believing that people are "born gay and cannot change." In fact, if the thought of anyone with same-sex attraction (SSA) changing his or her sexual attraction is not even on your radar screen, you have been misled.

We have failed to understand what same-sex attracted men and women are going through. In the past, many of us treated people who experience SSA unfairly. We may have taunted and teased them. We may have rejected and judged them: "You're going to hell for this." "You're a fag." "Somebody ought to beat the queer out of you!" Instead of listening, instead of trying to understand what they are experiencing, we have hurt already hurting people.

Meanwhile, homosexual activists have organized, planned, and strategized how to gain public acceptance. They've begun with the reality that everyone needs to belong; everyone needs to be loved. Capitalizing on those needs, in the course of recent decades they have created a movement of empowerment. "We're queer, we're here, get used to it" were the cries of ACT-UP in the 1980s. And by now we have gotten used to it. But should we?

Today teenagers are "coming out," declaring themselves to be homosexual earlier than ever before. More married men and women are announcing, "I am gay" to their spouses and children. The fight for homosexual marriage in the USA was achieved in June 2015 and in many other countries throughout the world. New homosexual legislation is changing the moral fabric of society. A multitude of major motion pictures, television shows, and made-for-TV movies sympathetically portray the lives of homosexual men and women while demonizing people of faith as ill informed and intolerant.

Regarding homosexuality, many religious denominations are divided over two challenging issues: (1) should they allow active "gay" clergy to pastor their churches, and (2) should they endorse homosexual relationships? *Basically, we are straight and late!* By that I mean most of us failed to demonstrate compassion and understanding to those who experience same-sex attraction, and we are coming to this realization after the issue has been forced upon us.

As a former homosexual, and as a psychotherapist, I know this issue from the inside out. For many years I struggled with unwanted SSA and then lived as a "gay" man. However, I had a burning desire in my heart to marry a woman and have children. Although the world told me that I was born with SSA and could not change, I never believed that. In my heart I knew that my destiny was to marry a woman and create a loving family. Today, I am living my dream. My wife and I have three incredible children. Our oldest son is a medical doctor; our daughter is an English teacher; and our youngest son is studying medicine. My dream is now a reality!

It is sometimes said, "Whoever frames the debate, wins the debate." In recent decades, the Gay Rights Movement has strategically moved the debate about homosexuality from the realm of psychology and morality, and brought it into the arena of human rights and social justice. Why did they do this? Because they were sick and tired of being treated like second-class citizens. Before the 1970s, they found little hope for acceptance and understanding in the religious community or mental health profession. Instead they suffered constant ridicule and judgment for their homosexual desires—desires they never asked for in the first place. They were trapped with their backs against the wall, hurting, angry, resentful, and alone. What could they do? Who would help them? In the pages that follow, I will try and bring clarity to these questions and many more.

- Chapter One: Brief history of the "Gay Rights Movement" and what motivates their every decision and action.

- Chapter Two: How homosexual feelings develop in men and women, the real meaning behind same-sex attraction.

- Chapter Three: Clues why five celebrities experience SSA: Olympic gold medal diver Greg Louganis, rock star Melissa Etheridge, former NBA player John Amaechi, talk show host and actress Rosie O'Donnell, and former U.S. Department of Education Safe School Czar Kevin Jennings.

- Chapter Four: Terminology coined by homosexual activists alongside suggested language than can bring greater healing to those who experience SSA.

- Chapter Five: Simple and effective ways to love those with SSA the right way, and thus help end the homosexual dilemma facing our nation and world.

This book is a basic primer about homosexuality. Consider it a Homosexuality 101 course. There are many other wonderful books on this subject listed in the back, which will give you an even deeper understanding about the causes behind same-sex attraction and the possibility of change.

I will repeat several concepts frequently throughout the book. Marketing strategies and psychological principles that are used to promote ideas on a daily basis impose beliefs upon us. For four decades, there has been one hand clapping regarding the issue of homosexuality. I would like to introduce you to the other hand! In so doing, I will repeat often, and in many similar ways, that *people are not essentially born with SSA*. I will say again and again that *they never simply chose to have homosexual feelings*, and that *changing from SSA to OSA (Opposite-Sex Attracted) is possible*.

In between the chapters you will find uplifting stories of transformation, demonstrating how a man or woman has made the change from homosexual to heterosexual desires. Through these narratives, you will come to understand more deeply the causes of SSA and how healing occurs. You may want to read all the chapters in the order presented, or reflect on them independently; it's entirely up to you. By the end I hope that you will have discovered how to love your SSA friend or family member in healthy ways.

Note: I use the term "gay" in quotes throughout the book as I view this as a socio-political term denoting someone who has accepted their SSA and decides to live a homosexual life. Also, the terms "lesbian, gay, bisexual, and transgender" (LGBT), are used for socio-political purposes.

I do not believe there is any such thing as a "homosexual," viewed as a noun. There are only people who experience SSA. I will continue to emphasize people who "experience same-sex attraction" as it is only an adjective describing their thoughts, feelings, and/or desires. It does not define who they genuinely are.

I will not use the concept "homosexual lifestyle," but living a homosexual life.

CHAPTER ONE

Brief History of the "Gay Rights Movement"

"Years of learning to hate myself didn't just slip away because I came out, and I still struggled with my feelings of self-loathing, feelings I would later come to understand as internalized homophobia. Unlike other traditional minorities in American society (Jews, people of color), gay people aren't raised by people like themselves and aren't connected to a community of people like themselves when growing up. As a result, we internalize the typically homophobic attitudes of those around us, and devaluing and demeaning homosexuality becomes part of our own self-image. This voice in your own head—the voice that constantly tells you that you are worthless—is the real enemy. Like a lot of gay people, I found that other people sometimes accepted me long before I had completely accepted myself" (*Momma's Boy, Preacher's Son,* Beacon Press, 2006, p. 121).

Kevin Jennings, Former Assistant Deputy Secretary,
Office of Safe & Drug Free Schools,
U.S. Department of Education

In this chapter, I will briefly detail the history of the Gay Rights Movement, expose the activists' strategic plan to normalize homosexuality in the USA and throughout the world, and disclose what fuels their agenda.

Prejudice against anyone who experiences SSA is wrong and needs to be corrected. However, embracing homosexual behavior as a normative condition is equally devastating. Why? Because it betrays the innate heterosexual potential of every precious SSA man and woman in this world.

Why, when, and how did the Gay Rights Movement come into existence? What is the motivation behind their movement? How did homosexual activists achieve so much in such a short period of time? We need to understand how these activists influence our daily lives through the scientific community, religious institutions, media and entertainment industries, educational system, and the political process. Many in the "lesbian, gay, bisexual, and transgender" (LGBT) community have enormous disposable incomes, as most of them do not have children. Money equals power!

Included in this chapter are the following topics:

- Historical Discrimination Leads to Guilt and Shame
- Birth of the "Gay Rights Movement"
- *After the Ball*, a Landmark Book that is Sometimes Called the "Homosexual Manifesto"
- Capturing the Scientific Community
- Religious Institutions Revise Theology: Historical Relativism
- Media and Entertainment Industry Promote Homosexuality
- Educational System Endorses LGBT Identity and Relationships
- Political Pressure to Enact Homosexual Legislation

Behind all the demands of homosexual activists are hurt little boys and girls who are longing for your love and acceptance. They never chose to experience SSA, and yet they incurred deep wounds when family, friends, and their community rejected them. What were they to do? Who would defend them? Feeling hurt and pain, they organized and mobilized. They did all of this to win your love.

Historical Discrimination Leads to Guilt and Shame

Men and women with Same-Sex Attraction are often…

- Rejected by Religions
- Rejected by Governments
- Rejected by Educational Systems
- Rejected by the Scientific Community
- Rejected by their Family Members and Friends

We know that throughout history many religions have been the greatest perpetrators of judgment and discrimination against men and women who experienced same-sex attraction. Churches, mosques and synagogues should have been the safest places for them, places of refuge and love, offering hope for healing. Instead, religious institutions were often appalling perpetrators of judgment and persecution toward those who experienced homosexual feelings. They quoted Leviticus 18:22 and Leviticus 20:13—homosexual acts are "detestable" and an "abomination"—while completely overlooking the fact that heterosexual behaviors outside of marriage are condemned in the same passages. This permitted people of faith to act self-righteously toward those who experience SSA.

The government also failed to protect SSA men and women, who often lost their jobs, homes, and lives. What about equal justice under law? What about the right to pursue life, liberty and happiness? Why were some men and women who experience SSA unfairly treated in their work place or even in the privacy of their own homes?

Within the educational system, there has long been discrimination against students and teachers who experience SSA. Many same-sex attracted youth have been bullied and even assaulted because of their homosexual feelings, while no school ordinances and very few administrators protected them.

The scientific community has, in fact, flip-flopped. Prior to the early 1970s, many therapists successfully treated men and women who experienced unwanted same-sex attraction, helping them achieve their heterosexual dreams. However, in 1973, first the American Psychiatric Association and then the American Psychological Association abdicated scientific facts under political pressure from homosexual activists both within and outside of their organizations. The scientific community truly failed the SSA population from that time on, caving in to the political pressure of the day (more details about this will soon follow).

Families also failed to understand, love, and support their SSA children and relatives. If a family member "came out," disclosing their SSA, often times they were ostracized and disowned, which left them with nowhere to go. The heart of the family is supposed to be a place of warmth, safety, comfort and love. When a family of a SSA child abandons her or him, s/he becomes an orphan left out in the cold.

Failure to love those who experience SSA by religious institutions, government agencies, educational systems, the scientific community, and their families fueled the birth of the Gay Rights Movement:

— "We're mad as hell, and we're not going to take it any more."

— "You've hurt us, not helped us."

— "All you did was condemn and mock us for feelings we never chose."

— "You say we're an abomination. You say that I can't live here. You say that I can't work here. You say I can't worship here. Where do I belong?"

Birth of the "Gay Rights Movement"

- Stonewall Riots in New York City
- Gay Pride Month
- Birth of Homosexual Organizations
- *After the Ball:* Homosexual Manifesto

What were they to do? Where were they to go? Who would protect and defend them? In the 1960s, on the coattails of the Civil Rights Movement in the USA, homosexual activism was born (although various homophile organizations began springing up in the 1950s, such as Mattachine Society and Daughters of Bilitis). On June 28, 1969, at about 1:20 a.m., at a homosexual bar called Stonewall Inn located in Greenwich Village, New York City, a historic event occurred, later to be known as the "Stonewall Riots."

The police regularly broke into homosexual bars, harassing and beating up the customers. Finally, after years of misuse and abuse, they had had it. In the early morning hours of June 28, the LGBT patrons essentially stood up and said, "We're here, we're queer, and we're not going to take it any more." They fought back. The battle between the Stonewall customers and police lasted for several days. This became the spark that lit the fire throughout the USA and created the Gay Rights Movement. In every major city throughout the world, June or July is celebrated as "Gay Pride Month" to commemorate the 1969 Stonewall Riots.

From that time they began to organize. Groups like The National Gay and Lesbian Task Force took shape. Many others soon followed: Lambda Legal Defense Fund (litigious arm of the homosexual movement), Human Rights Campaign (political action committee to change laws), and many more. They emulated strategies of the Civil Rights Movement, realizing they had to change public opinion about homosexuality in order to gain acceptance.

After the Ball, the Homosexual Manifesto

As this new homosexual rights movement gained momentum, activists got organized. In 1989 a remarkable book was published entitled *After the Ball: How America will conquer its fear and hatred of gays in the '90s* (all quotes used by permission from the publisher). Two "gay" men, Marshall Kirk and Hunter Madsen, wrote the book. Mr. Kirk was a researcher in neuropsychiatry, a logician, poet, and 1980 graduate from Harvard University. Mr. Madsen was an expert in public persuasion tactics and social marketing who designed commercial advertising on Madison Avenue; he graduated from Harvard in 1985.

In this landmark book, commonly known as the "Homosexual Manifesto," they mapped out a blueprint detailing how to indoctrinate the world into the innate-immutable mythology of homosexuality—"people are born gay and therefore cannot change." The authors clearly stated in *After the Ball* that they knew there is *insufficient scientific evidence that people are born with SSA*. Nonetheless, they decided to use this paradigm shift to gain public acceptance. This was their way of saying, "all is fair in love and war."

> The authors of *After the Ball* cleverly took the debate about homosexuality out of the realm of religion and psychology and brought it into the realm of human rights and social justice. "Whoever frames the debate wins the debate." They strategically took the emphasis off of *homosexual behavior*—anal sex, oral sex, mutual masturbation, fisting—and placed it solely on *homosexual identity*: "We are born gay; God made us this way; being gay is not just what we do, it is who we are."

The political venue, using their mantra of human rights and social justice, was virgin territory for the promotion of homosexuality and public acceptance. It was a stroke of genius to shift the debate about homosexuality away from religious beliefs and psychological evidence, and move it to the realms of human rights and social justice. There they could influence public opinion and gain acceptance.

After the Ball is a remarkable strategic plan to homosexualize the world. And in just a short period of time, the authors accomplished almost all of their goals. Let's look at the gist of their strategies:

"This is a campaign of unabashed propaganda, firmly grounded in long-established principles of psychology and advertising" (*After the Ball*, Marshall Kirk and Hunter Madsen, Plume Book, New York, 1989, p. xxviii).

The authors had to address a hostile public who feared and often hated persons who experienced homosexual feelings. It is interesting that in their book Kirk and Madsen used the word "homo-hatred" instead of homophobia. I prefer the term homo-hatred myself; I believe it is more accurate. Homo-hatred describes a person who either speaks against or acts disparagingly toward a person who experiences SSA. I do not hate or fear anybody who experiences homosexual feelings. On the contrary, I have the utmost love and respect for all SSA men and women. I simply believe that people are not born with same-sex attraction and therefore can change. I also believe that homosexual behavior is incompatible with natural law.

Homophobia is a misleading and inaccurate term; "phobia" represents an irrational fear of something or someone. Many of us do not fear or have prejudice toward people who identify as "gay." However, LGBT persons easily label anyone with a principled disagreement about homosexual behavior as "homophobic." This is incorrect based upon their own definition.

The authors discuss what most heterosexuals think about member of the LGBT community: "(1) hardly worth thinking about, (2) few in numbers, (3) easy to spot, (4) homosexual because of sin, insanity, or seduction, (5) kinky, loathsome sex addicts, (6) unproductive and untrustworthy members of society, and (7) suicidally unhappy" (p.61).

> Kirk and Madsen decided to portray homosexuality as a *condition*, not as a *problem*, because *a problem can be fixed, but a condition must be accepted*. This, again, was part of their strategic plan: Homosexuals are not broken, therefore, we should respect and accept them just as they are.

Madsen and Kirk realized that most people are extremely prejudiced against homosexuals and homosexual behavior. They analyzed the nature of prejudice—an illogical emotion, an automatic response to emotional conditioning, which is impervious to argument. Therefore prejudice is not a thought process, it is an emotion. In order for LGBT activists to be successful, they had to understand how prejudice works: (1) you can't argue it away, (2) it's not evil, (3) conscious raising won't work, (4) prejudice is not an illness so it can't be cured by therapy, (5) it's not a conspiracy by sick or wicked people, (6) homosexual parades where homosexuals look extreme will not work, (7) learning to love and respect others will not work, (8) storming the barricades or picketing these people will not work, and (9) having sex in public places certainly will not work (pp. 113-114). So how would they move people from prejudice against homosexuality to acceptance of it?

They describe how prejudice works as an evolutionary function for survival and reproduction, in other words "survival of the fittest." We fear that which we don't understand, we make snap judgments without thinking, and thus the fight or flight response ensues. Homo-hatred is basically a learned pattern. Therefore what was learned can be unlearned. Connections made in the brain can be broken down and new connections made. "Prejudice is not a belief; it's a feeling. Argument can change beliefs, but not feelings. It's not useful in the treatment of homo-hatred" (p. 136).

> "When you're very different, and people hate you for it, this is what you do: first you get your foot in the door, by being as similar as possible; then, and only then—when your one little difference is finally accepted—can you start dragging in your other peculiarities, one by one. You hammer in the wedge narrow end first. As the saying goes, Allow the camel's nose beneath the tent, and his whole body will soon follow" (p. 146).

Three-Stage Plan to Homosexualize the Nation:

(1) Desensitization

(2) Jamming

(3) Conversion

Kirk and Madsen declared that it is relatively easy to retrain the human brain to feel and react neutrally to a previously hated minority such as "lesbian, gay, bisexual, and transgender" persons. They developed a three-stage plan to accomplish this—Desensitization, Jamming, and Conversion.

First comes *desensitization*, which is the constant flooding of homosexual imagery into the culture through advertising, media, people sharing their stories, and homosexual related messages on a regular basis. This "flooding" of homosexual imagery will eventually desensitize us, until we think that homosexuality is just another "thing." "If straights can't shut the shower off, they may at least eventually get used to being wet" (p. 149). Today, everywhere you turn, there are images of LGBT persons on television, movies, Internet, newspapers, magazines, religion, science, schools, and politics.

Second is *jamming*, which can be thought of as throwing sand in a watch mechanism, and thereby preventing prejudice. "Jamming makes use of the rules of Associative Conditioning (the psychological process whereby, when two things are repeatedly juxtaposed, one's feelings about one thing are transferred to the other, e.g., picture-label pair) and Direct Emotional Modeling (the inborn tendency of human beings to feel what they perceive others to be feeling)" (p. 150). An example of picture-label pair would be Oprah Winfrey embracing Ellen DeGeneres. A person might think, "I don't like Ellen because she's a lesbian. But Oprah likes Ellen, and I like Oprah, so I guess I'll like Ellen."

"Our effect is achieved without references to facts, logic, or proof...through repeated infralogical emotional conditioning, his bigotry can be alloyed in exactly the same way, whether he is conscious of the attack or not" (pp. 152-153).

Third and last is *conversion*, where the wheels of the watch turn in the opposite direction. "We mean conversion of the average American's emotions, mind, and will, through a planned psychological attack, in the form of propaganda fed to the nation via the media. We mean 'subverting' the mechanism of prejudice to our own ends—using the very processes that made America hate us to turn their hatred into warm regard—whether they like it or not. Put briefly, if Desensitization let the watch run down, and Jamming throws sand in the works, Conversion reverses the spring so that the hands run backward" (pp. 153-154). This was their long-range goal, using the media to convert the public to full acceptance of homosexuality.

Most of us have been reprogrammed through this brilliant strategy. Here's how someone might unknowingly be reoriented through this reprogramming: "Well, I've learned that homosexuality is normal, people are born gay. I was the bigot. I contributed to their suffering. Now, I love Ellen DeGeneres. I think she's just great. I love Greg Louganis. I love Ricky Martin and Elton John. I love all gay people. I changed. All those religious judgments were lies that only hurt people. All gays and lesbians deserve the same rights as everyone else."

Kirk and Madsen continued to describe other methods to homosexualize every nation through a campaign of propaganda using eight principles of persuasion (pp. 173-191):

1 – Don't just express yourself: communicate!

2 – Seek ye not the saved nor the damned: appeal to the skeptics

3 – Keep talking

4 – Keep the message focused: you're a homosexual, not a whale

5 – Portray gays as victims, not aggressive challengers

6 – Give potential protectors a just cause

7 – Make gays look good

8 – Make victimizers look bad

Allow me to summarize these eight principles of propaganda so that you may comprehend how well conceived and executed their plan was:

Principle one—"Don't just express yourself, communicate!" Put yourself out there. Share your story. Make heterosexuals believe that you speak their language, look like them, act like them, and dress like them.

Principle two—"Seek ye not the saved nor the damned: appeal to the skeptics." There are "intransigents" that are against homosexuality and make up 30-35% of the population, usually the more religious types. Next are "friends" of homosexuals, who make up 25-30% of the population. Finally, there are "ambivalent skeptics," about 35-45% of the people. These ambivalent or skeptical people are the primary target of this campaign. They are the target audience.

Principle three—"Keep talking." Desensitize and share stories:

"You can forget about trying right up front to persuade folks that homosexuality is a good thing. But if you can get them to think it's just another thing, meriting no more than just a shrug of the shoulders, then your battle for legal and social rights is virtually won" (p. 177).

Keep talking, keep sharing, keep coming out, and let people know you are "gay." Use AIDS as a topic to emphasize discrimination: homosexuals deserve their civil rights, to be treated with dignity and respect. Regarding religious people with conservative beliefs: "Portray such institutions as antiquated backwaters, badly out of step with the times and with the latest findings of psychology" (p. 179). Talk in public; get on TV, into films, and magazines.

Principle four—"Keep the message focused: you are a homosexual, not a whale." Be single-minded: This is about gay rights and we have to talk about gay rights as much as we can, in as many venues as possible.

Principle five—"Portray gays as victims, not as aggressive challengers." "The purpose of victim imagery is to make straights feel very uncomfortable; that is, to jam with shame the self-righteous pride that would ordinarily accompany and reward their anti-gay belligerence, and to lay the groundwork for the process of conversion by leading straights to identify with gays and sympathize with their underdog status" (p. 183). Gays are "victims of circumstance" and "victims of prejudice" (p. 184). Help straights become protectors for the victims. "Persons featured in the media campaign should be wholesome and admirable by straight standards and completely unexceptional in all appearance; in other words, they should be indistinguishable from straights we'd like to reach" (p. 183).

"To suggest in public that homosexuality might be chosen is to open the can of worms labeled 'moral choice and sin' and give the religious intransigents a stick to beat us with. Straights must be taught that it is as natural for some persons to be homosexual as it is for others to be heterosexual: wickedness and seduction have nothing to do with it. And since no choice is involved, gayness can be no more blameworthy than straightness. In fact, it is simply a matter of the odds—one in ten—as to who turns out gay and who straight. Each heterosexual must be led to realize that he might as easily been born homosexual himself" (p. 184).

This is pure genius, normalizing homosexuality, making it equivalent to heterosexuality: according to this construction, you or I could have turned out "gay," "lesbian," "bisexual," or "transgender." In Chapter Two I will debunk this false notion.

Misinformation about population percentages was also introduced, creating yet another homosexual myth: "Ten percent of the population is gay." This has no basis in fact or scientific evidence. Although many people change their sexual behavior at various times in their lives, today, according to the latest research studies, it is estimated that perhaps 2-3% of the population live a homosexual life. "About 1.4 percent of the women said they thought of themselves as homosexual or bisexual and about 2.8 percent of the men identified themselves in this way....no matter how we define homosexuality, we come up with small percentages of people who are currently gay or lesbian" (*Sex in America: A Definitive Survey*, Robert T. Michael, John H. Gagnon, Edward O. Laumann, and Gina Kolata, Boston: Little Brown and Co., 1994, pp. 176-177). These results came from surveys conducted by the scholarly team at the University of Chicago, the National Health and Social Life Survey (NHSLS). Kirk and Madsen, along with other homosexual strategists, increased the percentage as yet another strategy to reclassify homosexuality as a substantial "minority" in search of acceptance.

Principle six—"Give potential protectors a just cause." Use anti-discrimination in the campaign against homo-hatred, show how homosexuals are being treated terribly. Anti-discrimination is the calling card.

Principle seven—"Make gays look good." Gays are victims. They are just like everyone else and more—they also need our protection. They need to create their own television shows and films. Make gays look good and have famous people endorse them.

Principle eight—"Make victimizers look bad." Make homo-hating beliefs and actions look so bad that everyone will dissociate from them.

> "The best way to make homo-hatred look bad is to vilify those who victimize gays. The public should be shown images of ranting homo-haters whose associated traits and attitudes appall and anger middle America" (p. 189).

The best example I've ever seen of this type of person is Fred Phelps. He is supposedly a Baptist minister, however, he and his followers preach and practice hate, and they have nothing to do with God and Biblical principles of love (leadership of the Baptist denomination have denounced Mr. Phelps). I personally have debated this man on radio. He is not a godly person. He and his followers attend LGBT marches and events such as Matthew Shepherd's funeral, carrying signs saying "God hates fags," and "God condemns you to hell." Phelps is a poster boy for homo-hatred. His approach leads members of the LGBT community to despise people of faith and, to defend homosexuals as victims of hate. Phelps ideally serves the purpose of principle number eight: to make victimizers look bad, creating more sympathy for their cause.

There you have it, the eight principles of propaganda to eliminate prejudice toward LGBT persons. Finally, the authors introduce three tactics to dominate the media: (1) public relations—keep getting the message out; (2) news reporting—make friends with people in the news business, call them, tell them about homosexual-related stories, take them out and befriend them; and (3) advertise—show that LGBT persons are just like everyone else, and spend time with people in the media. To accomplish this, the authors suggest using television, radio, magazines, newspapers, billboards, and display ads to disseminate their message.

I have been on numerous television shows, i.e., Larry King Live, O'Reilly Factor, 20/20, Jimmy Kimmel Live, CNN, Rachel Maddow Show, etc. Many members of these TV shows' staff (producers, directors, writers, editors, technicians, musicians), as well as the staff of other shows, are active members of the LGBT community. They write, produce, and direct the shows, and therefore easily control the message.

The authors' concluding comments explain how to keep the propaganda campaign alive:

> "You may discount what the pious tell you because it is actually rage, not love, that lay behind all those progressive events. Like all emotions, rage has its purpose and its time and its place. When a situation becomes intolerable and oppression unbearable, when millions do not even dare cry out beneath the heel of injustice, rage is the appropriate response" (p. 382).

This sums up Kirk and Madsen's homosexual manifesto. According to them, love will not help to achieve their equal rights. "Keep your rage burning! We must reverse the engine of prejudice using these tactics."

> *The motivation behind the Gay Rights Movement is pain, anger, and rage, which represent wounded souls in desperate need of love and acceptance. This is the fuel that drives their engines: "Accept me. Help me. I'm hurting. Please love me." Again, underneath all their demands are little children longing for love and acceptance.*

Capturing the Scientific Community

- Storming the Bastille of the American Psychiatric Association

- Revising Homosexual Diagnosis in the DSM/ICD

- Homosexual Therapists Rule Mental Health Organizations

Imagine there is a building with a pillar on each side (see the diagram). Let's call this building: *The Homosexual Movement.* The pillar on the left side of the building is: "We are born gay." The pillar on the right side of the building is: "We cannot change." This is the paradigm that shifted the entire homosexual debate—"born gay and cannot change." Here is how they achieved this masterful but false claim through the scientific community in the 1970s.

The Homosexual Movement

Before *After the Ball* was written, other homosexual activists were busy working to influence public opinion. They recognized that the "priests" of the 20th century were no longer religious leaders but members of the medical and mental health professions. If science said it, then it must be true. They set out to capture the scientific community in order to promote full acceptance of homosexuality.

From 1970 to 1973 LGBT activists pummeled psychiatrists of the American Psychiatric Association (APA) at their annual conventions. When a psychiatrist presented a paper about the etiology and/or treatment of ego-dystonic homosexuality (someone conflicted over their SSA), a "gay" activist would start screaming, jump on tables, and shout, "How dare you treat us like this? How dare you systematize prejudice? You are killing us. Stop killing us!" And all the while they were filling the air with obscenities.

They revealed their pain. They ripped open their chests and exposed their hearts: "We're mad as hell and we're not going to take it any more! Stop discriminating against us!" Their pain was palpable; however, they used it as a ploy to *force* psychiatrists to remove homosexuality as an illness from the Diagnostic and Statistical Manual of Mental Disorders (DSM). The DSM is the "bible" of diagnostic disorders that therapists and physicians use throughout the USA. (Most therapists and physicians worldwide use the International Classification of Diseases, known as the ICD).

Homosexual activists within and outside the APA started a letter-writing campaign to all the voting membership, imploring them to remove the diagnosis of homosexuality from the DSM. The National Gay and Lesbian Task Force funded this effort, as documented in Dr. Ronald Bayer's book, *Homosexuality and American Psychiatry*. (Ronald Bayer, professor at Columbia University, was previously at the Hastings Center, a research institute devoted to the study of ethical issues in medicine and the life sciences.) Members of the APA had no idea who was behind this letter writing campaign. A scientific issue became politicized overnight, part of the strategy by key LGBT activists.

In December of 1973, by a narrow vote, homosexuality was removed from the DSM. The vote was not based on scientific research but on political pressure from homosexual activists. Dr. Bayer wrote,

"Instead of being engaged in a sober consideration of data, psychiatrists were swept up in a political controversy. The American Psychiatric Association had fallen victim to the disorder of a tumultuous year, when disruptive conflicts threatened to politicize every aspect of American social life…The result was not a conclusion based on an approximation of the scientific truth as dictated by reason, but was instead an action demanded by the ideological temper of the time" (*Homosexuality and American Psychiatry*, Ronald Bayer, Princeton University Press, Princeton, NJ, 1981, pp. 3-4).

Following the narrow vote to remove homosexuality from the DSM, newspapers worldwide reported, "Doctors declare homosexuality normal," even though the psychiatrists did not say that. That is how "gay" activists spun this decision. It was a coup d'état. The APA was kidnapped by LGBT activists.

Science went out the window and politics came in the door. Since that time therapists were discouraged from discussing the potential causes and the successful treatment of unwanted same-sex attraction in any mental health organization, including the American Psychiatric Association, American Psychological Association, American Counseling Association, American Medical Association, and all other professional organizations. They all drank the Kool-Aid.

Those professionals who offer research on the causes and treatment of unwanted same-sex attraction are labeled "homophobic," "anti-gay," and publicly humiliated—so much for "tolerance, diversity, and equality," the mantra of the "Gay Rights Movement." In fact, true tolerance is a two-way street where diverse opinions are heard and respected. The decision by the APA in December of 1973 created a new mentality regarding homosexuality in the mental health profession: If it ain't broke, then you don't have to fix it. However, it took other countries more than a decade to adopt the same position and remove homosexuality from the ICD.

Dr. Robert Spitzer, professor of psychiatry at Columbia University, was a key player in this whole APA phenomenon that took place in the early 1970s. He was the chair of the nomenclature committee that was investigating whether or not to remove homosexuality from the DSM. After much debate, he advised them to remove it. Now fast-forward thirty years: in October 2003, Dr. Spitzer published a study in the *Archives of Sexual Behavior* about 200 men and women who changed from a homosexual to a heterosexual orientation. He acknowledged that these changes had, in fact, taken place. Can you imagine the outrage of homosexual activists? Dr. Spitzer received hate mail, threatening phone calls, and others tried to have him fired from his position as professor of psychiatry at Columbia University. He wrote an Op Ed piece for the *Wall Street Journal* and said, ladies and gentlemen, we are scientists and have the right to investigate phenomena. Let's cut the politics. We have a scientific obligation to discuss all issues. However, in 2013 Spitzer caved into political pressure by LGBT activists and wrote an apology for his study in The New York Times. However, this public apology does not invalidate the findings of his study. I was one of the participants, and at least a dozen of my formal clients. Additionally, I know approximately one hundred of the participants who are all living happy, heterosexual lives. The study is valid!

Today almost all mental health organizations promote what is called "gay affirmative therapy." In undergraduate and graduate psychology courses, there is rarely a discussion about the etiology and/or treatment of unwanted SSA. Students in counseling programs are taught gay affirmative therapy, hardly aware of the possibility of change. In some universities, psychology students have been expelled from their program because they refused to counsel "gay" identified clients or couples based on their religious beliefs. In other states and countries, teachers were fired because they would not affirm homosexual behavior based on spiritual convictions. To cite one example, Julea Ward was expelled from her graduate counseling program at Eastern Michigan University in March 2009, because she said that she was unable to counsel a homosexual couple because of her religious beliefs.

When a client comes in for treatment and has unwanted homosexual feelings, or does not want to accept his or her homosexuality, the new diagnosis is "internalized homophobia." The majority of trained professional therapists today instruct all SSA clients to accept themselves as "gay," without a mention about the possibility of change. If the parents and family members do not accept their child's homosexuality, they are shamed, and they too are classified as having "internalized homophobia." The parents, family members, or friends who cannot accept their loved ones homosexual identity or behavior are considered part of the problem, and they are shamed into changing their views.

The American Psychological Association in 2007 created a task force to study sexual reorientation therapies that help those who experience unwanted SSA fulfill their heterosexual potential. This committee consisted of strictly gay-identified therapists and those who support homosexuality. The APA refused to allow any sexual reorientation therapists on this task force. Their results were predictable: this type of therapy is contra-indicated. In other words, it doesn't really work. But if one carefully reads their results, they stated that the studies showing evidence of change were not rigorously conducted. That means they are not sure if this type of therapy works. So much for the client's right of self-determination. Again, politics trumped science.

Religious Institutions Revise Theology: Historical Relativism

- Historical Relativism, Revisionist or Pro-Gay Theology
- Religions Divided Down the Middle
- Para-Church Ministries Reach Out to Those Who Experience Unwanted SSA

In today's religious community, there is a great divide over homosexuality:

Side one: "Homosexuality is sinful, it's an abomination. We reject homosexual people."

Side two: "Homosexuals are wonderful! We endorse their homosexual identity and homosexual behavior."

Proponents of homosexuality within the religious community have reinvented theology. Their position is called "historical relativism," "revisionist theology" or "pro-gay theology." They base their "gay" theology on three principles: 1) many past Biblical prohibitions are no longer valid today, 2) Scriptures regarding homosexual behavior did not include committed "gay" couples, and 3) authors of the Bible did not have the latest scientific facts, that people are born "gay." These three principles are the basis for "gay theology."

The two polar attitudes—endorsing and condemning homosexuality—miss the mark entirely. We need a paradigm shift, a centrist view that states:

"If you experience SSA, God loves you and we love you too. You are welcome here. We do not approve of any sexual behavior outside of marriage between a man and a woman. We believe that you were not essentially born with same-sex attraction. And God loves you, and so do we. We embrace all people. You are welcome in our synagogue, in our church, in our mosque."

We need to be protectors of those who experience SSA and offer them unconditional love along with truth and healing. We need to separate the person from their behavior. *Scripture does not speak negatively about people who experience SSA in either the Old or New Testament.* All Scriptures refer to homosexual behavior, as well as heterosexual behavior outside of marriage. There is no condemnation for people who experience SSA.

Most religious denominations are divided straight down the middle when it comes to the homosexual issue, debating whether or not to ordain active homosexual clergy and/or marry homosexual couples. These two divisive issues confront every religion worldwide, wreaking havoc and shattering peoples' faith. "Did God make people gay?" "Are they truly born this way?" "Should we revisit and revise what the Bible actually says about homosexual behavior being sinful?" LGBT persons are challenging traditional faith and Biblical views of homosexuality. Episcopalians, Anglicans, Lutherans, Methodists, Presbyterians, Catholics, Baptists, Mormons, Jews, Hindus, and other faiths are equally divided on this issue. Muslims still disapprove of homosexual behavior, although it is quietly practiced in all Islamic countries.

Although many denominational doctrines promote a Biblical view of sexuality—marriage is meant for one man and one woman, and all sex outside of marriage is incompatible with God's design for human sexuality—they are daily conforming to a changing social trend of the acceptance of homosexuality, and incorporating those beliefs into church and/or religious doctrine. "Revisionist theology" is the fashion of the day—old ways are not applicable to new understandings, therefore, we must yield to a more modern view.

Many religions have two para-church organizations:

(1) LGBT groups which endorse homosexual behavior.

(2) Groups that assist men and women who experience unwanted SSA.

Catholic: Dignity (pro-homosexual) vs. Courage (healing homosexuality)

Episcopal: Integrity (pro-homosexual) vs. none

Methodist: Reconciling Ministries (pro-homosexual) vs. Transforming Congregations (healing homosexuality)

Presbyterian: More Light Presbyterians / Covenant Network of Presbyterians (pro-homosexual) vs. One By One (healing homosexuality)

Mormon: Affirmation (pro-homosexual) vs. North Star (healing homosexuality)

Jewish: Many pro-homosexual Jewish groups vs. Jewish Institute for Global Awareness

Historically most people of faith treated men and women who experience SSA abominably. Now, instead of repenting to these men and women on bended knees, many religious groups are throwing the baby out with the bathwater—revising theology without truly understanding what drives homosexual behavior. Instead of learning more about same-sex attraction, they are succumbing to political pressure and following social trend by endorsing homosexual behavior. Everyone is losing. Although members of the LGBT community think they are finally getting what they want, will this tactic truly give them what they need?

Media and Entertainment Industry Promote Homosexuality

- Television Shows Created By LGBT persons
- LGBT Moguls Rule Hollywood
- News and Cable Shows with Pro-Homosexual Views

Several years ago my wife and I were guests on the Montel Williams Show. An openly "gay" staff member met us at the train station. I asked him, "Do you know why we are here?" He said, "Oh yes, and I have contacted members of the gay and lesbian communities in both New York and New Jersey to be in the audience." It turned out that the show was an ambush, meant to denigrate me as well as the other guests who spoke a loving message about the possibility of coming out of homosexuality.

This experience has become daily diet for those of us who promote the possibility of changing from same-sex attracted (SSA) to opposite-sex attracted (OSA). Over the past twenty-five years I have been on countless TV shows, done hundreds of radio interviews, and have been written about in newspapers and magazines worldwide. I have seen the power of "gays" in the media, mostly behind the scenes, setting the agenda for national dialogue. In 2000, when I released my first book, *Coming Out Straight: Understanding and Healing Homosexuality* (about the causes and healing of unwanted SSA), I hired a publicist to help promote the book. I hired her because she was "gay-affirming" and no one in the media would accuse me of being "anti-gay." She had connections with all the major TV shows in the USA. She was confident that she could help garner interviews on the most important morning and prime time talk shows.

She soon found one door after another closing in her face! "Richard, I have tried my best. I have to say in all honesty, I was the bigot. At first, I thought that I could not work with you because you were anti-gay. But, actually, I was the one who was prejudiced, and not you. I experience you as a loving, caring, and genuinely compassionate man." She continued, "I was dumbfounded that the so-called 'liberal media' is so intolerant! They are completely closed to your view. I have done my best and failed. I'm sorry."

Each year on the Oscars, Golden Globes, and Emmys, which are broadcast on television worldwide, we see many "gay" and "lesbian" actors accept awards. They kiss their partners; they publicly thank their partners, and many allude to the glories of being "gay" and the need for more acceptance. This is just another means of normalizing homosexual behavior and gaining public acceptance.

Again we return to the Homosexual Manifesto's commission to members of the LGBT community: "Tell your stories to the media, say them loud and clear, be convincing, be a victim and gain heterosexual's support." This has been accomplished. Many in the LGBT community hold powerful positions in Hollywood and in the media.

Television:

> **Sex and the City**: Creator, Darren Star
>
> **Desperate Housewives**: Creator, Marc Cherry
>
> **Will & Grace**: Creators, David Kohan & Max Mutchnick
>
> **Glee, American Horror Story**: Creator, Ryan Murphy
>
> **Looking**: Creator Michael Lannan
>
> **Queer as Folk**: Creator Russell T. Davies
>
> "Gay" men created all of these television shows. What do they have in common? Often the male characters are weak and the women are strong. This mirrors many "gay" men's family of origin—weak or absent fathers and domineering mothers. Additionally, most LGBT relationships presented on these TV series are failed; they don't work and end in heartbreak. We don't see happy "gay" couples, only sad ones. And today most television shows and movies have an LGBT character. It's the new norm.

At the beginning of all Dreamworks films is their trademark, a little boy sitting on the moon fishing. Below are the initials SKG, which stand for Steven Spielberg, Jeffrey Katzenberg, and David Geffen.

Mr. Geffen (with an estimated net worth of almost five billion dollars) is a record executive, film and theatrical producer. A "gay" man, he has tremendous power and influence in Hollywood and politics. He has donated millions of dollars to various political campaigns as well as to HRC and other homosexual organizations (more about HRC and other homosexual political groups later).

Geffen serves as just one example of innumerable LGBT persons in powerful positions, who are crafting the message for an unsuspecting public. The fact is that many people in front of and behind the camera on television and films are framing the debate and discussion about homosexuality—"gay is good," "those who seek change or promote this opportunity are bad," and "those who do not fully accept homosexuality are 'homophobic,' 'anti-gay,' ignorant people." Most movies and television shows sympathetically portray LGBT men and women and demonize anyone who disagrees with their behavior.

Educational System Endorses "Gay" Identity and Relationships

- Gay Straight Alliance (GSA) in Public Schools
- Gay Lesbian Straight Education Network (GLSEN)
- Health Curricula Revised: "Born Gay and Cannot Change"

Many years ago, in my eldest son's high school, there was a Gay Straight Alliance (GSA). A GSA club enters public and private schools under the guise of protecting LGBT students, and very quickly turns to the promotion of homosexuality. These groups impugn the integrity of anyone who disagrees with their beliefs. I saw this firsthand in my son's high school. Any student who has a different viewpoint about homosexual behavior, based on religious, spiritual, or psychological views, is called names and discriminated against. Where is the tolerance? Where is the diversity of opinion? Where is the equality?

There are thousands of GSAs in middle and high schools across the USA and around the world, initiated by the Gay Lesbian Straight Education Network (GLSEN) founded by Kevin Jennings in 1990. Kevin's autobiography, *Mamma's Boy, Preacher's Son*, recounts his horrific experiences from elementary through high school, being ridiculed and mocked by fellow students while being unprotected by teachers and school administrators. I will share an evaluation of why

I believe Kevin Jennings experiences SSA in Chapter Three. From 2009 – 2011, he served as the Assistant Deputy Secretary for Safe and Drug-Free Schools under the U.S. Department of Education in the Obama administration. He was essentially the "Safe School Czar," dictating public policy and protecting LGBT students from being bullied. He attempted to heal the hurt that he and so many other SSA children experienced when they were in school. But while he may be creating a safer environment for them, he was at the same time betraying the very essence of their true gender identity. More about this in the next chapter.

Mission of GLSEN: "The Gay, Lesbian and Straight Education Network strives to assure that each member of every school community is valued and respected regardless of sexual orientation or gender identity/expression. We believe that such an atmosphere engenders a positive sense of self, which is the basis of educational achievement and personal growth." "Currently, GLSEN has registered more than 4,000 GSAs, has approximately 40 full-time staff, a governing board of 20 members and two advisory committees at the national level" (http://www.glsen.org/cgi-bin/iowa/all/about/history/index.html). GLSEN believes in respect for those who agree with them, but treats those with differing views as hostile and unacceptable, calling them derogatory names.

Children's books like *Heather Has Two Mommies, Daddy's Roommate,* and *Gloria Goes to Gay Pride* are just a few examples of how children in elementary school are being enrolled into believing the homosexual myth. Movies such as *It's Elementary* (shown in public and private schools around the nation and on television) are also soliciting children into this false ideology. Sensitivity trainings for schoolteachers further their cause. Most school libraries carry books promoting homosexual behavior while completely ignoring the reality that there is another side to this issue.

Health curricula taught to elementary, middle, and high school students in many communities throughout the country and world also include teaching on homosexuality—basically, "people are born gay and cannot change." I saw this first hand in my younger son's health classes when he was in middle school. These curricula are not scientifically valid, yet they are being used to propagandize future generations with false information about homosexuality (desensitize, jam, convert). If remained unchallenged, our children will become puppets of a propaganda machine as well as future voters, endorsing homosexual behavior because they know nothing other than the homosexual myth, "born gay and cannot change."

Political Pressure to Enact Homosexual Legislation

- Human Rights Campaign (HRC)
- Lambda Legal
- Parents and Friends of Lesbians and Gays (PFLAG)
- National Gay and Lesbian Task Force
- Gay and Lesbian Alliance Against Defamation (GLADD)

Members of homosexual organizations are driven by their hurt, pain, and a need for belonging, acceptance and love. Homosexual organizations founded in the USA fund and educate homosexual groups worldwide. They have taught and continue to mentor new organizations about how to achieve acceptance in the fields of science, religion, education, media, entertainment, and politics.

The world's largest homosexual *political action committee* is the **Human Rights Campaign (HRC).** Their annual budget is well over a $40 million. They have a national headquarters building located at DuPont Circle in the heart of Washington, D.C., with a full-time staff of over 100, and thousands of volunteers around the USA and in many countries throughout the world. They work in the political arena for "gay rights legislation" (www.hrc.org), to enact homosexual legislation on the federal, state and local levels.

Many years ago I spoke at a church in St. Paul, Minnesota. Over 300 people attended. About one-third of the audience was either "gay" identified or were LGBT activists, many of whom wore apparel from the Human Rights Campaign (they have a recognizable logo with a blue background and yellow equals sign in the middle). To say that the HRC representatives were upset when I shared my belief, that people are not essentially born with SSA and that changing from same-sex attracted to opposite-sex attracted is possible, would be an understatement. This is so because their lives are predicated on the innate, immutable paradigm—*born with SSA, cannot change.*

During the question and answer session following the talk, many wanted my head on a chopping block. Instead, I offered them love and compassion, agreeing to disagree, showing them the face of true tolerance and real diversity. *Love is the greatest medicine to heal all pain.*

HRC is active and on the move from city-to-city, state-to-state, and government-to-government. I have debated several HRC staff members on various television and radio interviews. They are polished and professional, showing a pleasant and amiable face to homosexuality, as taught to them in the Homosexual Manifesto. They work tirelessly to transform legislation to incorporate homosexual behavior into every city, state, and federal law. Be aware, changes are happening daily unbeknownst to most of us (see the list below of homosexual leaders within the United States federal government).

Lambda Legal is a litigious organization that challenges and sues states and federal government's laws pertaining to homosexual behavior, as well as supporting other homosexual activities worldwide (www.lambdalegal.org). Most LGBT legal victories within the USA have either been won in the courts or through legislation, and more recently through popular vote. HRC influences legislators while Lambda Legal works within the court system.

Parents and Friends of Lesbians and Gays (PFLAG) (www.pflag.org) promotes homosexuality throughout the country. They have over 350 chapters in 50 states with over 200,000 members. PFLAG vision: "We, the parents, families and friends of lesbian, gay, bisexual and transgender persons, celebrate diversity and envision a society that embraces everyone, including those of diverse sexual orientations and gender identities. Only with respect, dignity and equality for all will we reach our full potential as human beings, individually and collectively. PFLAG welcomes the participation and support of all who share in, and hope to realize this vision" (http://community.pflag.org/Page.aspx?pid=237).

I found this a bit contradictory since I have participated in several PFLAG meetings, at which I was mocked and ridiculed for my personal and professional beliefs about homosexuality—no one is born this way and change is possible. My colleagues and I have discovered that tolerance from LGBT organizations goes something like this: "My way or the highway!" PFLAG members visit public schools under the guise of non-discrimination, and promote total acceptance of homosexuality with total disregard for other views. They are wonderful and good-hearted people who are simply ignorant about the facts of SSA.

Other significant and powerful homosexual organizations:

National Gay and Lesbian Task Force (www.thetaskforce.org): "The mission of the National Gay and Lesbian Task Force is to build the grassroots power of the lesbian, gay, bisexual and transgender (LGBT) community. We do this by training activists, equipping state and local organizations with the skills needed to organize broad-based campaigns to defeat anti-LGBT referenda and advance pro-LGBT legislation, and building the organizational capacity of our movement. Our Policy Institute, the movement's premier think tank, provides research and policy analysis to support the struggle for complete equality and to counter right-wing lies. As part of a broader social justice movement, we work to create a nation that respects the diversity of human expression and identity and creates opportunity for all" (http://www.thetaskforce.org/about_us/mission_statements).

Gay and Lesbian Alliance Against Defamation (GLAAD) (www.glaad.org): "The Gay & Lesbian Alliance Against Defamation (GLAAD) is dedicated to promoting and ensuring fair, accurate and inclusive representation of people and events in the media as a means of eliminating homophobia and discrimination based on gender identity and sexual orientation" (http://www.glaad.org/mission). GLAAD activists serve as media watchdogs and come down hard on anyone who does not agree with promoting homosexuality. Yes, protection is necessary, but they don't provide the whole picture. In their perspective, no other opinion is acceptable. After I participated in an interview on CNN in April 2010, GLADD attacked CNN for allowing me to share my viewpoint. In fact, the majority of coverage on CNN, along with most other cable and network television news, promotes only homosexual views. Again, where is the diversity? Where is their tolerance? What about equality?

Apart from these non-governmental agencies stands the most powerful entity of all—the USA Federal Government. As of April 2010, here is a list of the LGBT men and women in the US federal government who influence public policy and laws that govern our nation. Today, there are even more LGBT persons in prominent government positions (source: Gay and Lesbian Leadership Institute at www.glli.org/presidential):

- **Mark Agrast** - Deputy Assistant Attorney General, Office of Legislative Affairs at the Department of Justice

- **Raul Alvillar** - Congressional Relations Officer, Housing and Urban Development

- **Judy Applebaum** - Deputy Assistant Attorney General, Office of Legislative Affairs at the Department of Justice

- **Cynthia Attwood** - Member, Occupational Safety and Health Review Commission

- **Vic Basile** - Senior Counselor to the Director, Office of Personnel Management

- **Anthony Bernal** - Scheduler, Office of Dr. Jill Biden

- **Jeremy Bernard** - Director of White House and Congressional Affairs, National Endowment for the Humanities

- **John Berry** - Director, Office of Personnel Management

- **Jeremy Bishop** - Special Assistant to the Secretary, Office of Public Engagement at the Department of Labor

- **Brian Bond** - Deputy Director, White House Office of Public Engagement

- **Raphael Bostic** - Assistant Secretary for Policy Development and Research, Housing and Urban Development

- **Ebs Burnough** - Deputy Social Secretary, Office of the First Lady

- **Michael Camunez** - Assistant Secretary for Market Access and Compliance, Department of Commerce

- **Lyle Canceko** - Deputy Director, Center for Faith Based and Neighborhood Partnerships, Department of Commerce

- **Jamison Citron** - Confidential Assistant, Office of White House Liaison, Department of Health and Human Services

- **Brook Colangelo** - Chief Information Officer, White House Office of Administration

- **John Connor** - Director, Office of White House Liaison at the Department of Commerce

- **John Coppola** - Member of the National Museum and Library Services Board

- **Jeffrey Crowley** - Director, Office of National AIDS Policy

- **Fred Davie** - Member, President's Advisory Council on Faith-Based and Neighborhood Partnerships

- **Justin DeJong** - Deputy Press Secretary, Department of Agriculture

- **Marisa Demeo** - Associate Judge, DC Superior Court

- **Jenny Durkan** - U.S. Attorney, Western District of Washington

- **John Easton** - Director, Institute of Education Sciences

- **Eric Fanning** - Deputy Under Secretary of the Navy

- **Chai Feldblum** - Equal Employment Opportunity Commission

- **Carl Fillichio** - Senior Advisor to the Secretary of Labor for Public Affairs and Communications

- **Daniel Gordon** - Administrator for Federal Procurement Policy, OMB

- **Kathy Greenlee** - Assistant Secretary, Administration on Aging, Department of Health and Human Services

- **Steve Gunderson** - Member, President's Commission on White House Fellows

- **David Hansell** - Principal Deputy Assistant Secretary for Children and Families, Administration for Children and Families

- **Emily Hewitt** - Chief Justice, U.S. Court of Federal Claims
- **Jennifer Ho** - Deputy Director, Accountability Management at the U.S. Interagency Council on Homelessness
- **Fred Hochberg** - Chairman, U.S. Export-Import Bank
- **David Huebner** - U.S. Ambassador to New Zealand
- **Glenda Humiston** - State Director for Rural Development in California
- **Shin Inouye** - Director, Specialty Media
- **John Isa** - Deputy Executive Director, Federal Office of Compliance
- **Karine Jean-Pierre** - Regional Director, Office of Political Affairs
- **Kevin Jennings** - Deputy Assistant Secretary, Office of Safe and Drug-Free Schools
- **Kristina Johnson** - Under Secretary, Department of Energy
- **Jenn Jones** - Special Assistant, Department of Housing and Urban Development
- **Elaine Kaplan** - General Counsel, Office of Personnel Management
- **Brad Kiley** - Director, White House Office of Management and Administration
- **Harry Knox** - Member, President's Advisory Council on Faith-Based and Neighborhood Partnerships
- **Kei Koizumi** - Assistant Director for Federal Research and Development, Office of Science and Technology Policy
- **Andy Lee** - Chief of Staff, Office of Innovation and Improvement at the Department of Education
- **Jeffrey Lerner** - Regional Director, Office of Political Affairs

- **Sara Lipscomb** - General Counsel, Small Business Administration
- **Zach Liscow** - Staff Economist, Council of Economic Advisers
- **Thomas Lopach** - Senior Vice President, Congressional Affairs, U.S. Export-Import Bank
- **Sharon Lubinski** - U.S. Marshall
- **John Marble** - Public Affairs Specialist, Office of Personnel Management
- **Jeffrey Marburg-Goodman** - Special Counsel to the USAID Administrator
- **Mercedes Marquez** - Assistant Secretary for Community Planning and Development, Department of Housing and Urban Development
- **Kathy Martinez** - Assistant Secretary for Disability Employment Policy, Department of Labor
- **Michael Martinez** - Special Assistant, National Resources Conservation Division, USDA
- **Mary Beth Maxwell** - Senior Advisor, Department of Labor
- **Philip McNamara** - Executive Secretary, U.S. Department of Homeland Security
- **David Medina** - Deputy Chief of Staff, Office of the First Lady
- **David Mills** - Assistant Secretary for Export Enforcement, Department of Commerce
- **Alison Nathan** - Associate Counsel to the President, White House Counsels Office
- **Jeffrey Neal** - Chief Human Capital Officer, U.S. Department of Homeland Security

- **Ven Neralla** - Director of Priority Placement, Presidential Personnel

- **Dave Noble** - White House Liaison, National Aeronautics and Space Administration

- **Matt Nosanchuk** - Senior Counselor to the Assistant Attorney General for Civil Rights, Department of Justice

- **Dylan Orr** - Special Assistant to the Assistant Secretary of Labor, Office of Disability Employment Policy

- **Joseph Palacios** - Board of Visitors for WHINSEC

- **Paolo Palugod** - Special Assistant to the Assistant Attorney General for the Environment and Natural Resources Division, DOJ

- **Peter Pappas** - Chief Communications Officer for the United States Patent and Trademark Office, Department of Commerce

- **Raul Perea-Henze** - Assistant Secretary of Policy and Planning, Department of Veterans Affairs

- **Drew Perraut** - Policy Analyst, Office of Information and Regulatory Affairs, OMB

- **Mark Perriello** - Director of Priority Placement, Presidential Personnel

- **Gautam Raghavan** - Deputy White House Liaison at the Department of Defense

- **Peter Roehrig**- Special Assistant, Office of Energy Efficiency and Renewable Energy

- **Constance L. Rogers** - Deputy Solicitor for Energy and Mineral Resources at Interior

- **Donna Ryu** - U.S. Magistrate Judge for the U.S. District Court for the Northern District of California

- **Ellie Sue Schafer** - Director, White House Visitors Office

- **Tarak Shah** - White House Council on Environmental Quality

- **Amanda Simpson** - Senior Technical Advisor to the Department of Commerce, Bureau of Industry and Security

- **Richard Sorian** - Assistant Secretary for Public Affairs, HHS

- **Campbell Spencer** - Regional Director, Office of Political Affairs

- **Everette Stubbs** - Deputy Director, White House Visitors Center

- **Nancy Sutley** - Chair, White House Council on Environmental Quality

- **Jonathan Swain** - Assistant Administrator, Small Business Administration

- **Kenneth Tolson** - Member, President's Board of Advisors on Historically Black Colleges and Universities

- **Moe Vela** - Director of Operations, Office of the Vice President

- **Alex Wagner** - Special Assistant to the Assistant Secretary of Defense for Global Strategic Affairs

- **Douglas B. Wilson** - Assistant Secretary of Defense for Public Affairs, Department of Defense

- **William Woolston** - Staff Economist, Council of Economic Advisers

Conclusion

As I re-read this chapter, which briefly traces the history of the homosexual movement, pain gripped my heart. How sad and unjust are the terrible ways that same-sex attracted men and women have been treated throughout history so often by their families, in their places of worship, in their schools, and in their neighborhoods. My heart breaks for each of them, because I used to be one of them. And yet, I know by pursuing acceptance through revisionist theology, compromised science, media spin, and special legislation, they will never experience the love and peace they so desperately seek and deserve.

> *The goal of this book is to promote real change and true love for all who experience SSA, so they can find warm and welcoming places in their families, places of worship, workplace, and communities.*

Who or what is the real enemy of the LGBT community? Is it a person or people? Is it parents who cannot endorse their child's homosexual behavior? Is it religious institutions that still hold sacred traditional Biblical principles? Is it a therapist who helps those who experience unwanted SSA? No. *The real enemy is ignorance and fear.* Because of very real discrimination, LGBT activists created a brilliant strategic plan to gain acceptance. Yet this plan was based on a false paradigm to persuade people that they were born with SSA, cannot change, and therefore everyone must love and accept them just as they are. This paradigm has worked. But the biggest losers are the men and women who may get everything they think they want, but will be denied what they truly need.

In summary, laws are being challenged and changed daily. Homosexual marriage is marching from country to country. The educational system has become more tolerant and sensitive to LGBT students while falsely teaching pro-homosexual lessons through health education curricula. Religious institutions continue to revise their faith traditions in order to accommodate "gay" identified men and women. Media and movies are basically the sound stage to promote homosexuality unchallenged, without debate. Scientific organizations are reluctant to allow any discussion about the causes and treatment of unwanted same-sex attraction.

We can and must reverse this through education and understanding. Allow me to offer a new perspective about homosexuality—where it actually originates. But first, let's hear from someone who experienced unwanted SSA and made a remarkable transformation to marriage with kids! In his own words, please enjoy Joseph's story.

Joseph's Story

In this book, I am including stories of three men and one woman who came out of homosexuality. My intention is to help you better understand the meaning behind same-sex attraction and the process of change. After each story, I will describe why I believe the writer experienced SSA. I'll also suggest how family and friends might help such individuals discover their innate heterosexual potential. Through this I hope you will acquire practical ideas how to assist anyone who experiences SSA, whether they wish to change or not. Learning to love the right ways will help all who experience SSA.

First is Joseph's story. He was my client for two years.

I was born in Europe. I lived there for more than twenty years. Thinking back always brings to mind the image of not having a particularly happy childhood. I was a very sensitive child, and so the confrontation with reality was much more difficult for me than it was for others. I can't tell exactly when I started to feel attractions towards boys. Several years ago, I realized that my uncle sexually abused me. I spent much time with him when I was three to five years old. When I first retrieved these memories, I felt terrified to remember the actual events that happened. What were more painful and intense were the feelings connected with the abuse, all the feelings that were stored in my body and mind for so many years. I virtually re-experienced the feelings that I had as a boy. Believe it or not, I am very happy to have had this memory, to know about it, because it is one factor that led to my homosexual desires.

My mother was at home with my brother and me. When I was a toddler, she did not give me the opportunity to break away from her and find my own way. I was educated to be the good boy! My father worked a lot and was seldom home; therefore no one was around to balance my mother's role in my life. My brother was born when I was nine years old. From the time of his birth, I was very jealous because I felt that he was the main focus of the family.

Growing up as a teenager was a good time for me because I had lots of friends in school, but at home I was still unhappy. My friends became my family, and I had sexual encounters with some of my male friends. Mutual masturbation and oral sex were the things we did together, and I started to like it. Around the same time, I found my father's pornographic magazines, and masturbation became more and more like a friend in my lonely life at home.

I never understood why I felt attractions towards boys and men. I felt it was one of the biggest burdens in my life because I also liked being with women, and I definitely wanted to have a family. After finishing high school, my life became even more confused. A good friend of mine went into the gay lifestyle. I didn't know if I should do the same.

At the same time, I was in love with a girl that somehow protected me. I still felt confused, but a trip to the U.S.A. helped to clarify my life and dreams. During the visit, I stayed with a gay couple. Through spending time with them, I realized that the gay lifestyle was absolutely *not* right for me. This helped define my dreams, but I still felt attractions towards men. In a way, it was more difficult now because I knew for sure that I did not want to go into the gay lifestyle.

At that time, I started to act out. I had sex with men in public parks and bathrooms. Even though it did not happen so often, it still gave me the feeling that I could meet my need for intimacy with men. It did not take too long before realizing how terrible the whole situation was. I tried to stay away from acting out as often as I could. I was partially successful because I relied more on masturbation, using gay pornography to calm down my need for male intimacy.

At this time, I was studying at a university. A friend helped me a lot. Through her, I heard about a therapist who specialized in helping people who experienced unwanted homosexual feelings. I finally met him during one of his seminar tours through Europe. For the first time in my life, I talked to someone about my problems and homosexual desires. Richard was very understanding and helpful. He explained to me the root causes of this condition. He told me that there was the possibility of healing. At that point, I had hope again. God, who helped me to get through all those painful years, had given me a wonderful gift!

My plan was to go to America and receive therapy. A year after I met Richard in Europe, I came to the U.S.A. There I went into therapy with a colleague of his. It was great because, for the first time, I could really share my story. I felt understood and not alone for the first time in my life.

After a couple of months in the States, I had to return to Europe to finish school. I also started to prepare to return for a longer period of time to receive more therapy and join a support group. Back at home, I had wonderful friends who totally supported me and especially a close friend of mine who knew my story, and he literally was there for me whenever I needed him. He held me when I needed healthy touch. Additionally we played sports together. We had fun and worked on different projects at our college campus.

At the time, I also met my wife-to-be, and I told her from the very beginning about my homosexual attractions. She said, "We will master it together!" She accompanied me back to the States. I started therapy with Richard and joined his support group. I also found a healing partner, which helped a lot. It was sometimes tough, but I learned more and more about myself. I discovered my inner child through various techniques that Richard taught me. This helped incredibly to heal the wounds of my past. Additionally, I used bioenergetics to release a lot of anger and pain stored in my body and soul.

Today, I have come a long way. Quite infrequently I experience attractions towards men. I learned it is just an indication that I am not caring for myself properly. When I address the issue, the attractions go away instantly. I feel very good, and I see that I grow closer to my wife every day. I am grateful to God to have had this opportunity to heal. I am grateful to those who pioneered this way of resolving unwanted homosexual feelings.

Comments

I worked with Joseph for two years. He made tremendous progress in that time. One of the most important parts of his therapy was learning about his inner child. Joseph not only had problems with compulsive masturbation and anonymous sexual behavior, he also had an eating disorder. Food and sex were his way of medicating his pain. Food and sex were love to him.

When he did the inner child workbook, he discovered a whole new world. Because of his devotion to his healing work, the voice within began to disclose more and more about his past and present situation. Joseph became a good parent to his inner family. The more he listened, the more he learned. Because of this and his healing relationships with other men, the homosexual desires naturally dissipated.

Joseph also had to learn a marvelous new word, which had not been a part of his vocabulary in either English or his native tongue. That word was "No." As he stated, he grew up being a "good boy" for his mommy and others. In his recovery work, he did a lot of bioenergetics—a scientifically proven therapeutic technique to help release pent up anger and pain—to reawaken his masculine energy.

When he finally got the hang of it, Joseph cut loose, and oceans of rage and pain were released. The support group was of tremendous benefit to him. Also, he was a gift to the group, as he readily shared himself with others. In this way, he mentored the newcomers.

Toward the end of our therapeutic relationship, Joseph invited his entire family over to America for a family healing session. It lasted one day, and it was simply magnificent. He was able to share with his mom and tell her how much pain he experienced by her overprotective nature. They wept together. She apologized, not realizing that what she had done had hurt her son so deeply.

He held his father, crying the tears of a child who so longed for his father's affection and attention. He told his dad how much he missed him when he was out working and in the pubs at night with his friends. "Why didn't you ever take me with you to work?" They, too, wept. His father apologized, and finally Joseph felt his strong daddy's arms around him. Now, their relationship is deepening with each visit. Joseph has requested that his mother back off for now so that he and his dad can bond.

Another amazing event took place during the family healing session. Joseph was able to apologize to his younger brother for the abusive way that he had treated him because of the intense jealousy he experienced. His brother expressed his pain, screaming about what he had gone through. They held each other, grieving together and reconnected in heart. Finally, his younger brother shared with Mom and Dad how their fighting hurt him. The entire family held each other, all in tears, releasing years of unexpressed pain. It was a new beginning for this family. Today, Joseph is more and more in love with his wife. Their sex life is great, his same-sex desires are gone, and they have three beautiful children. Joseph has now become a mentor and coach for men who experience unwanted same-sex attraction.

Conclusion

As you read Joseph's story, were you able to understand some of the reasons why he experienced SSA? In the next chapter, I will give a more detailed explanation of what contributes to the development of same-sex attraction in men and women. Here's a quick overview of Joseph's challenges:

1. Joseph experienced insufficient bonding with his father, and therefore was unable to incorporate his dad's masculinity and feel his own maleness. A boy first gets his sense of gender identity from his father. Joseph missed this important stage of psychosexual development.

2. Joseph was overly attached to his mother, internalizing her femininity. Many SSA boys were too close to their moms and too distant from their dads. This precludes them from experiencing their own male gender identity. Instead, they over-identify with women and/or the feminine.

3. Joseph, along with many SSA boys and girls, was highly sensitive, or hypersensitive. This temperament led to his acute feelings of being rejected by his father and being different from others.

4. Joseph developed the habit of acting like a pleaser. Many, who experience SSA, because they are highly sensitive, use their talents and gifts to win people's love. Joseph worked to obtain good grades, and to be an excellent student.

5. Joseph experienced sexual abuse by his uncle when he was three-to-five years old. This created a neurological pattern equating male sexual behavior with receiving love and attention. Joseph's father was absent from his life, so the relationship with his uncle became a substitute for male attention.

6. In puberty, the normal needs for pre-adolescent male bonding became sexualized. At first Joseph resisted and felt guilty. However, there was hole in his soul, a normal need to belong to the world of men, and sex became his substitute for healthy male bonding. The pattern of anonymous sex in Joseph's life served several purposes: (1) here Joseph showed up as real, no longer the "nice boy," but rather getting down and dirty, something he never allowed himself to be in real life, a powerful man, and (2) he used sex to experience some form of connection with men, that which was lacking in his early years of child development, being disconnected from his father.

Suggestions

Once we understand the dynamics that can lead to SSA, we can develop a list of ways family and friends can help:

1. Fathers, bond with your sons. Mothers, bond with your daughters. A child experiences the fullness of his or her own gender identity by successfully internalizing their same-sex parent's love. Even if your child has a different type of personality or temperament, it is still essential that they bond with you, and thereby incorporate either your maleness or femaleness. You are the primary source of gender identity for your son or daughter. Therefore, join in their world first, understand how they experience life, and then you can bring them into your world. Dads, do activities with yours sons, and moms, do things with your daughters. Keep it in mind that kids who are most likely to develop SSA are highly sensitive, and therefore will easily withdraw. Pursue them with unconditional love.

2. Guys, embrace other guys. Women, embrace other women. The second source from which we gain a sense of our gender

identity in pre-adolescence is through hanging out with and connecting to those of our same sex—guys with guys, and girls with girls. If this doesn't happen in those formative years of development, then people who acquire same-sex attraction may spend the rest of their lives looking for that sense of connection through homosexual relationships. However, the original need is that of a child and/or pre-adolescent, to feel a sense of belonging with those of the same sex.

3. In this case, Joseph needed male mentors to embrace him, to introduce him into the world of men. He experienced sexual abuse at an early age. The pattern of sexualizing relationships with men developed due to the lack of bonding with his father. The antidote to this is having male mentors and buddies reach out to the sensitive boys, showing them healthy male affection and acceptance, teaching them the ways of men. This will save these sensitive souls from a lifetime of seeking love through sexual activities.

4. Oftentimes, when a man who experiences SSA gets into a close relationship with a healthy, heterosexual men, his homosexual feelings subside. However, underneath his SSA, the wounds that created those desires still remain, and these will eventually need to be addressed and resolved. The natural process of healing is grieving the losses of one's past. What was created in unhealthy relationships needs to be healed in healthy relationships. Therefore, allow the SSA man to release his anger, hurt and pain from past relationships—hurts like the lack of father-son connection, sexual abuse, rejection by male peers, and over-attachment with mother. When the heart is heard and healed, then one's SSA will wane and opposite-sex desires are able to naturally arise.

Constellation of Potential Variables Creating Same-Sex Attraction

Heredity
- Inherited wounds
- Unresolved family issues
- Misperceptions
- Mental filters
- Predilection for rejection

Temperament
- Hypersensitive
- High maintenance
- Artistic nature
- Gender-nonconforming behaviors; Male more feminine; Female more masculine

Hetero-Emotional Wounds
- Enmeshment
- Neglect
- Abuse
- Abandonment
- Addictions
- Imitations of behaviors
- Wrong sex

Homo-Emotional Wounds
- Neglect
- Abuse
- Enmeshment
- Abandonment
- Addictions
- Imitations of behaviors
- Wrong sex

Sibling Wounds / Family Dynamics
- Put-downs
- Abuse
- Name calling

Body-Image Wounds
- Late bloomer
- Physical disabilities
- Shorter
- Thinner
- Larger
- Lack of coordination

Sexual Abuse
- Homosexual imprinting
- Learned and reinforced behaviors
- Substitute for affection

Social or Peer Wounds
- Name calling
- Put-downs
- Goody-goody
- Teacher's pet
- Non-athletic
- No rough and-tumble (boy)
- Too rough and-tumble (girl)

Cultural Wounds
- Media
- Educational system
- Entertainment industry
- Internet
- Pornography

Other Factors
- Divorce
- Death
- Intrauterine experiences & influences
- Adoption
- Religion

The severity of wounding in each category will have a direct impact on the amount of time and effort it will take to heal.

© Richard Cohen, M.A., 2010

CHAPTER TWO

Homosexuality: Born, Bred, or Both?

A re people born with SSA? Are homosexual feelings the result of genes, hormones, or biological differences? In this chapter we will compare the homosexual myth—"*born gay and cannot change*"—with scientific research and theory. What you will come to understand is that SSA is a symptom of three things:

(1) Innate temperament

(2) Wounds that haven't healed

(3) Unmet needs for love

As we have learned, LGBT activists spent many years and numerous resources promoting the homosexual myth. Trying to turn the wheel of propaganda is not easy, but facts are facts and the truth will ultimately be known.

In the world today, there are two prevailing views regarding homosexuality: the essentialist claims that people are born this way, while the constructionist says it is basically an acquired condition. We know that SSA is a bio-psycho-social phenomenon. Anyone claiming that people are simply "born gay" is misleading you by spinning inconclusive and faulty research.

Over the past several decades, many "gay" researchers have tried to prove that people are born with SSA. Their data is inconclusive, has not been replicated, and in most cases is easy to debunk. If you wish a more detailed scientific evaluation of why people are *not* born with SSA, please read *My Genes Made Me Do It!* by Dr. Neil and Briar Whitehead (free download available at www.mygenes.co.nz).

Previously, the American Psychological Association said that homosexuality was inherently innate. However, in 2008 they finally recanted and agreed with what the scientific research really showed:

"Although much research has examined the possible genetic, hormonal, developmental, social, and cultural influences on sexual orientation, no findings have emerged that permit scientists to conclude that sexual orientation is determined by any particular factor or factors" (http://www.apa.org/topics/sorientation.html).

In this chapter, we will explore:

• Biological and Genetic Studies about SSA

• Hidden Meaning Behind SSA

• Ten Potential Causes of SSA

• Seven Stages of "Coming Out"

• Coming Out Straight *is* Possible

Biological, Genetic, and Hormonal Studies about SSA

The Homosexual Movement

While studies, which try to purport a genetic, biologic, or hormonal basis for SSA, continue to emerge, no simple explanation will materialize because our sexuality is influenced by many factors. As we will learn, SSA develops through childhood and early adolescence, when the individual's brain and character have yet to reach full maturity. This is one explanation of why we may see the brains of those with SSA not fully actualized with their own gender identity. Also, through scientific studies, we know that the structure of the brain and chemistry of the body are changed by repeated behaviors. Therefore, in many studies, rather than observing the *causes* of homosexual feelings in men or women, we most likely are observing the *effects* of homosexual behavior upon their physiology.

1 – <u>No one is essentially born with same-sex attraction (SSA).</u>

There is no compelling scientific evidence that anyone is determined from birth to have SSA. There is no conclusive scientific data that proves there is a simple biological, genetic, or hormonal cause for homosexuality.

2 – <u>No one simply chooses to have SSA.</u>

Same-sex attractions are generally the result of unresolved childhood wounds and unmet needs for love. Homosexual desires arise from a combination of temperamental, environmental, and psychological issues (see the ten potential causes of SSA).

3 – <u>People may decide to resolve unwanted SSA.</u>

Research, along with my personal and professional experiences, demonstrates that change is possible. Men and women worldwide have transitioned from same-sex to opposite-sex attractions. Since no one is essentially born with SSA, change is possible.

In our culture and world today, there are many terms loosely used to define someone who experiences SSA: homosexual, bisexual, transgender, gay, and lesbian. Once again, the term "gay" is a socio-political term, which generally applies to an individual who identifies him or herself as accepting of their SSA, and therefore acts upon those desires. Lesbian refers to a woman who experiences SSA. Bisexual applies to someone who experiences both same-sex and opposite-sex attractions. Transgender describes those who believe they were born the wrong sex and wish to live life as the opposite gender. Members of the gay rights movement constructed the term "sexual orientation." We shall discuss these and other terms in Chapter Four.

There are also those who experience unwanted same-sex attraction and do not identify themselves as "gay," "lesbian," "bisexual," "transgender," or homosexual. There are young children who experiment with those of the same sex during the onset of adolescence and puberty, as boys are closer to boys at this stage of development, and girls are closer to girls. This does not make them a person who experiences SSA. There are others who engage in homosexual practices during other stages of their life and move on, for example male students in boarding schools. Likewise, there are men and women who, while incarcerated, engage in homosexual acts but revert to their heterosexuality upon leaving prison. It is only in the last century that we have resorted to labeling people and practices. It is important to remove these labels and understand what drives human behaviors, especially those who experience obligatory same-sex attraction.

Since the early 1990s, the myth of the "gay gene" and "homosexuality is biological" was promoted throughout the media. A few well-publicized studies launched this campaign to indoctrinate an unsuspecting public into believing that people are born this way and therefore cannot change (as we've seen, these are the two pillars of the LGBT movement). Since then, more studies have appeared trying to prove the "born gay and cannot change" theory. Again, what we are most likely observing are not the causes of SSA, but rather the results of homosexual behavior upon the brain of active SSA men and women.

Dr. Kenneth Klivington, researcher at the Salk Institute in San Diego, CA, stated, "There is a body of evidence that shows the brain's neural networks reconfigure themselves in response to certain experience. Therefore, the difference in homosexual brain structure may be a result of behavior and environmental conditions" (David Gelman et al., "Born or Bred," *Newsweek*, February 24, 1992, p. 46).

Dr. Ruth Hubbard and Dr. Elijah Wald of Harvard University state in their 1993 book, *Exploding the Gene Myth,* "The myth of the all-powerful gene is based on flawed science that discounts the environmental context in which we and our genes exist" (p. 6).

Here are three studies conducted in the 1990s used to advance the homosexual myth in courts and legislative bodies to enact homosexual laws worldwide. With the exception of J. Michael Bailey, these researchers are "gay" identified:

Dr. Simon LeVay conducted a study entitled, "A Difference in Hypothalamic Structure between Heterosexual and Homosexual Men," *Science,* August 30, 1991 (Vol. 253, pp. 1034-1037). He observed the brains of men who had died: 19 "gay" subjects and 16 heterosexual subjects. He professed to have found a group of neurons in the hypothalamus (called INAH3) that appeared to be twice as large in the heterosexual men as in the homosexual men. LeVay theorized that this part of the hypothalamus has something to do with sexual behavior. Therefore, he concluded that sexual orientation is somehow biologically determined. Upon a closer look at his findings, we see many contradictions:

(1) All 19 "gay" subjects in the study died of AIDS. We know that HIV/AIDS affects the brain causing chemical changes. Therefore, we may be observing the effects of HIV/AIDS on the brain, not the cause of SSA.

(2) Regarding his so-called heterosexual subjects, LeVay states, "Two of these subjects (both AIDS patients) had denied homosexual activity. The records of the remaining 14 patients contained no information about their sexual orientation; they are assumed to have been mostly or all heterosexual" (Ibid, p. 1036). Can you really assume someone is heterosexual

because their medical records didn't specify their sexual proclivity? This is hardly science!

In his article, "Salt and Pepper" in the *Bay Area Reporter*, Michael Botkin—homosexual AIDS activist and psychotherapist—stated, "It turns out that LeVay doesn't know anything about the sexual orientation of his control group, the 16 corpses 'presumed heterosexual.' A sloppy control like this is…enough by itself to invalidate the study. LeVay's defense? He knows his controls are het[erosexual] because their brains are different from the HIVer corpses. Sorry, doctor; this is circular logic. You can use the sample to prove the theory or vice versa, but not both at the same time" (September 5, 1991, pp. 21, 24; Source: http://www.leaderu.com/marco/special/spc10.html).

(3) Three of the 19 homosexual subjects had a larger group of neurons in the hypothalamus than the average heterosexual subject. Three of the 16 heterosexual subjects had a smaller group of neurons in the hypothalamus than the average homosexual subject. Six out of 35 subjects disproved LeVay's hypothesis. The results are not statistically significant; they cannot be related to the general population. In order for a study to be seen as valid and reliable, a high enough percentage of subjects must prove the author's theory. This study should never have been published, a fact which many scientists affirmed in the months following its publication.

(4) Finally, LeVay himself stated he did not prove that people are born with SSA: *"It's important to stress what I didn't find. I did not prove that homosexuality is genetic, or find a genetic cause for being gay. I didn't show that gay men are born that way, the most common mistake people make in interpreting my work"* ("Sex and the Brain," *Discover*, Vol. 15, no. 3, March 1994, pp. 64-71).

A twin and sibling study was conducted by J. Michael Bailey and Richard Pillard entitled, "A Genetic Study of Male Sexual Orientation." It was published in the *Archives of General Psychiatry*, Vol. 48, December 1991. They observed the prevalence of homosexuality among twins and adopted brothers where at least one brother was same-sex attracted. They found that 52 percent (29 pairs out of 56) of the identical twins were both SSA; 22 percent (12 pairs out of 54) of the fraternal twins were both SSA; and 11 percent (6 of 57) of the adoptive brothers were both SSA. They also found 9 percent (13 of 142) of the non-twin biological siblings were both SSA. The authors then concluded that there must be a genetic basis for SSA. Let us take a closer look and separate fact from fiction:

(1) The biggest flaw is the interpretation of the researchers. Since approximately 50 percent of the identical twins were not SSA, we may easily conclude that genetics does not play a significant role in their homosexuality. If it had, then 100 percent of the twins should be SSA since identical twins have the same genetic makeup. We might just as easily interpret the findings to mean that environmental influences caused their homosexuality. Biology professor and self-proclaimed lesbian Anne Fausto-Stirling of Brown University stated, "In order for such a study to be at all meaningful, you'd have to look at twins raised apart. It's such badly interpreted genetics" (David Gelman et al., "Born or Bred?" *Newsweek*, February 24, 1992, p. 46).

(2) This was not a random sample, but a biased sample, as the twins who volunteered for this study were solicited through advertisements in LGBT newspapers and magazines as opposed to general periodicals. If the authors had acquired their subjects from the general population, the percentage of brothers experiencing SSA would have been much smaller.

The researchers skewed the data to make it say what they wanted it to say.

Australian researchers observed 33,000 pairs of identical twins from a national database and found that when one twin was SSA, the other twin was SSA only 11% of the time (**Journal of Personality and Social Psychology**, (2000), 78 (3), 524-536).

(3) Dr. LeVay, author of the previous study, stated, "In fact, the twin studies…suggest that it's not totally inborn [homosexuality], because even identical twins are not always of the same sexual orientation" (Quoted in Marlin Maddoux, *Answers to the Gay Deception*, Dallas, TX, International Christian Media, 1994, p. 26).

(4) Dr. Bailey, one of the researchers, stated, "There must be something in the environment to yield the discordant twins" (Gelman, *Newsweek*, 1992, p. 46).

Finally, Dean Hamer and associates from the National Cancer Institute released a study, "A Linkage between DNA Markers on the X Chromosome and Male Sexual Orientation," *Science*, July 16, 1993, Vol. 261, pp. 3212-3217. The media reported immediately that the "gay gene" was discovered. Sorry to disappoint, even Dr. Hammer confessed this was false.

The researchers studied 40 pairs of homosexual brothers and suggested that some cases of homosexuality are linked to a specific region on the X chromosome (Xq28) inherited from the mother by her SSA son(s). Thirty-three pairs of the brothers shared the same pattern variation in the tip of one arm of the chromosome. Hamer estimated that the sequence of the given genetic markers on Xq28 is linked to homosexuality in 64 percent of the brothers. Let's see if his theory holds up under scientific scrutiny:

(1) There was no control group. Hamer and associates failed to test the heterosexual brothers of these SSA men. What if they have the same genetic markers as their SSA brothers?

(2) No one has even proven that the identified section of the chromosome has a direct relationship to sexuality or sexual proclivity.

(3) One of Hamer's research assistants accused him of withholding some of the findings that would have invalidated his study. We have never heard the end result of this investigation by the National Cancer Institute (John Horgan, "Gay Genes, Revisited," *Scientific American*, November, 1995, p. 26).

(4) A group of researchers from the University of Western Ontario under the guidance of Dr. George Rice conducted a study using the same scientific protocol and were unable to produce the same result. ("Where Did the Gay Gene Go?" www.abcnews.com, April 23, 1999).

(5) Hamer himself declared, "These genes do not cause people to become homosexuals…ultimately it is the environment that determines how these genes will express themselves" (*Time*, April 27, 1998, pp. 60-61).

Again, all these researchers, except for J. Michael Bailey, are self-proclaimed "gay" men. They desperately seek acceptance, and it is their conviction that if we believe they are "born" with SSA, then we must legitimize their homosexual behavior. Instead, we need to reveal the truth behind the homosexual myth, to discover what really causes people to experience same-sex attraction. Here is a more accurate analysis:

The American College of Pediatricians released a fact sheet about youth in April 2010 stating, "Homosexuality is not a genetically-determined, unchangeable trait. Homosexual attraction is determined by a combination of familial, environmental, social and biological influences. Inheritance of predisposing personality traits may play a role for some. Consequently, homosexual attraction is changeable." (www.FactsAboutYouth.com)

Meaning Behind SSA

Meaning Behind Same-Sex Attraction (SSA)

1. Homosexuality is a symptom of
- Unhealed wounds of the past (ten potential causes)
- Unmet needs for love
- Reparative drive to fulfill homo-emotional and/or homo-social love needs

2. Homosexuality is essentially an emotionally-based condition
- Need for same-sex parent's / same-sex peers' love
- Need for gender identification
- Fear of intimacy with members of the opposite sex

3. SSA represents a lack of gender identity, caused by either:
- Detachment from same-sex parent
- Detachment from same-sex peers
- Detachment from one's body
- Detachment from one's own gender

© Richard Cohen, M.A., 2010

As you will soon discover, there are many contributing factors that lead a boy or girl to develop homosexual feelings. Many professional therapists and I have observed that, most often, SSA men and women are highly sensitive or hypersensitive individuals. Therefore, they experience life situations and relationships more deeply than other children. This temperament of hypersensitivity often leads these boys and girls to *perceive* rejection from their parents, from their peers, from other family members and friends. This perception becomes their reality: "I don't fit in. I'm different. I don't belong." These are the core beliefs of most children and adolescents who experience SSA.

If you are a parent of a SSA child, please do not blame yourself. This is not a blame game. What we hope to identify here is what may have occurred for the sole purpose of healing and reconciliation. Knowledge is power. Understanding the deeper meaning behind homosexual feelings is instrumental to bring about lasting change.

---

1. Homosexuality is a symptom of:

- Unhealed wounds of the past (see ten potential causes chart)

- Unmet needs for love

- Reparative drive to fulfill homo-emotional and/or homo-social love needs

---

Homosexual feelings, thoughts, and desires are always symptoms of underlying issues. They represent (1) a defensive response to conflicts in the present, a way to medicate pain, (2) unresolved childhood trauma, archaic emotions, and wounds that never healed, and (3) a *reparative drive* to fulfill homo-emotional love needs (bonding with the same-sex parent, i.e., father-son, mother-daughter) and/or homo-social love needs (bonding with the same-sex peers, i.e., guys with guys, girls with girls).

By "reparative drive" we mean that the individual who experiences SSA is seeking to experience the love he or she did not attain in early childhood and adolescence, and is doing so by trying to connect with someone of the same sex. This reparative drive is most often completely unconscious. Dr. Elizabeth Moberly coined and Dr. Joseph Nicolosi further developed the concept of homo-emotional love need (read *Homosexuality: A New Christian Ethic* by Moberly and *Reparative Therapy of Male Homosexuality* by Nicolosi).

---

2. Homosexuality is essentially an emotionally-based condition:

- Need for same-sex parent's / same-sex peers' love
- Need for gender identification
- Fear of intimacy with members of the opposite sex

We gain our sense of gender identity—masculinity for a man, and femininity for a woman—through successful bonding with our same-sex parent and then same-sex relatives and peers. Most case histories of those who experience SSA demonstrate that homosexual feelings originate in early childhood and preadolescence.

From the ages of one or one-and-a-half to three, the child begins to crawl, walk and talk. This stage of development is known as a time of separation and individuation. The child begins to realize that she or he is different from mom, that she or he is an individual, separate and unique from mother. This time is known as either the terrible or terrific twos, and the operative word is, "No!" "No" essentially means that "I am not you, I am me, and I'm different from you." However, the boy has an extra developmental task here. He comes to realize that his genitals are different from his Mother's. Who does he look like, who does he resemble?

The boy must then gender identify with his father, his role model of masculinity. If the father is absent, another male mentor may help stand in the gap for the son. If there is no strong male presence in the toddler's life, he may continue to gender identify with his mother, internalizing her sense of femininity. This is one reason why many men who experience SSA may say, "From the time I was a child, I experienced homosexual feelings." They never successfully individuated from their mothers and gender identified with their fathers. On the other hand, the daughter, even though she is separating and individuating from her mother, will continue to gender identify with mom as her primary role model of femininity. She individuates while continuing to emulate her mother's behaviors. In the case of a potential SSA daughter, she may have been fearful of or repelled by her mother, and therefore didn't successfully internalize her own sense of femaleness (see other causes listed below).

Same-sex attraction often represents a search for parenting—a man seeking paternal love in the arms of another man, and a woman seeking maternal love in the arms of another woman (of course, this drive may be completely unconscious). It may also represent a need for bonding with same-sex peers because these men and women never experienced successful bonding with those of the same sex in their preadolescent and/or adolescent years of development. Then, during puberty, those normal needs for bonding, with same-sex parent and/ or same-sex peers, became sexualized and/or eroticized. At this point the world says to such a person, "You're born gay," or "You're born lesbian." This is a false label.

Labeling people with words like gay, lesbian, bisexual, or transgender is not only false, it also is done without a proper understanding of the situation. We are born as a man or a woman, as a son or a daughter. Those who experience SSA are merely stuck in early stages of psychosexual development. When they resolve past issues and fulfill unmet love needs in healthy, nonsexual, same-sex relationships, they will naturally develop opposite-sex desires. We are all heterosexually designed (men and women fit together beautifully and perfectly, biologically two men or two women simply do not).

If a man seeks to join sexually with another man, it means there is something lacking within him. He does not experience the fullness of his own masculinity. By joining with a man, he hopes to complete this lost part of himself. The same holds true for the woman seeking to join sexually with another woman. These yearnings represent the deep need of a child within—a need to experience love and secure bonding with someone of the same sex, to restore this lack of love. However, sexual relations will never satiate that need for love because it is that of a child, and children do not want or need sex.

In many cases men who experience SSA have been over-attached to their mothers and detached from their fathers and the masculinity they represented. As a result of closeness to his mom and detachment from his dad, the son becomes internally more feminine in nature. In adulthood, this may block his ability to have a successful heterosexual relationship with another woman, because of this over-attachment and identification with the feminine (remember, opposites attract). The same may hold true for the daughter who is over attached to her father and disconnected and dis-identified with her mother. She internalizes her dad's masculinity and rejects her mother's femininity. She may spend the rest of her life looking for that lost love and sense of connection with the feminine in the arms of other women.

Many women who experience SSA have been detached from their mothers, sexually/physically/emotionally/mentally abused by men, rejected by female peers, and/or are highly sensitive. Not wanting to re-experience abuse with men, many turn to other women for affection, comfort, and love. It is interesting to note that there is a higher percentage of domestic violence among lesbian couples than there is with heterosexual couples. Why? Underneath the exterior of these women are hurt little girls who were violated, who take out their aggression and unresolved pain on each other.

The father of Susan, an SSA woman, had had many affairs. He was loud, angry, judgmental, and strict. Susan developed anxiety around her dad as well as other men, and therefore turned to women for her affectional needs, seeking safety in their arms. Another SSA woman, Crystal, had parents who were always busy. She felt invisible to them. She clung to her brothers for attention and affection, even though they mistreated and abused her. Crystal fears revealing her heart to anyone, and longs for a woman to just hold her in her arms. You will also learn about another woman who experienced SSA, Debora, whose story appears after Chapter Three.

Psychotherapist Janelle Hallman, in her landmark book, *The Heart of Female Same-Sex Attraction* (InterVarsity Press, 2008), mentions four types of profiles of women who experience SSA. "They are primarily descriptive in nature and should *not* be rigidly construed: indeed, many women *may* identify with one profile over another, but will most likely see parts of themselves in each of the other profiles as well" (p. 159).

"Profile 1: Empty, Depressed, Withdrawn and Isolated. These women often have profound developmental deficits arising out of perceived and actual emotional absence or neglect. Their basic physical needs were met, but they nevertheless internalized the message that their existence was an inconvenience and a nuisance. Their lives are severely empty and lonely. They have a few friends, but the friendships lack mutuality. They feel more attached to objects or animals than to people. They are uncomfortable in their own skin and know that they are not 'normal,' at least in social settings. They may show marked inability to follow standard social cueing or comprehend—let alone articulate—inner emotional or psychological dynamics. They are often overweight and tend to be nondescript in appearance" (p. 160).

"Profile 2: Tough, Angry, Sarcastic and Barricaded. These women often have the worst histories of trauma and abuse, frequently involving severe physical or emotional abandonment, although this is not always the case. For some, the environments in which they were raised were not hostile, but the women nevertheless sensed and were negatively affected by the underlying relational dysfunctions within the family system. Both groups of women carry a deep belief that the world is not safe. They have relied on toughness (rather than the deadness found among profile 1 women) to protect their tender hearts. They are often overwhelmingly disillusioned to discover that their method of survival—severe defensiveness—actually starves them of intimacy. Unlike those associated with profile 1, they can feel their inner agony and therefore aggressively and continuously 'cut off' all vulnerabilities. They work hard but are demanding; they are impatient but also deeply committed. If they decide that you are safe, they will do anything in the world for you. They have an endless ability to care and take care of others, all the while denying their own needs" (p. 165).

"Profile 3: Energetic, Caretaking, Drama-Oriented, and never 'Home.' Even though these women are less likely to have typical trauma or neglect in their background as compared to women associated with profiles 1 and 2, they still suffer from severe, subtle and negative relational dynamics such as familial enmeshment or rigid gender roles within their families of origin. Due to their attuned sensitivities and perhaps their deeper relational needs, they felt that they were neither acknowledged nor affirmed as special, particularly as a girl. Although they felt close and loved, they also felt obligated to support or take care of other family members, including Mom and Dad. Nevertheless, their basic needs were usually met, and they experience the greatest level of stability among the four profiles. They are active, often athletic and typically overachieving women" (p. 170).

Profile 4: Pragmatic, Perfectionistic, Distant and Smugly Self-Assured. Women with this profile have various backgrounds but typically compensate for their losses and defend against their pain by avoiding all vulnerability and identifying with their ability to pursue excellence and success. They are often the movers and shakers within their field of expertise and find their kudos through achievement. They are very intelligent and extremely gifted. But because they are often so accomplished, they are also arrogant and contemptuous of others (especially men). They may unconsciously use others to serve their own purpose or meet their own needs" (p. 176).

Ms. Hallman concludes by appealing to her reader: *Please do not reduce a SSA woman to one profile. There is more to her than a simple description. The only useful purpose of these categories is to learn how to assist each woman in her healing process.* I hope you'll read Janelle's book for a more comprehensive understanding of female homosexuality.

---

3. SSA represents a lack of gender identity, caused by either:

- Detachment from same-sex parent
- Detachment from same-sex peers
- Detachment from one's body
- Detachment from one's own gender

Same-sex attractions may represent detachment between the individual and his or her same-sex parent and/or same-sex peers. Because the boy did not successfully or sufficiently bond with his dad and/or other male peers, he then rejects his own gender identity, not wanting to act or be like his father or other boys. After this occurs and puberty sets in, his emotional needs for bonding become sexualized. This is the construction of SSA and perhaps a "gay" identity—little boys and girls in adolescent or adult bodies looking for bonding through sexual relationships. Sexual behavior cannot and will not resolve their wounds and unmet love needs.

Ten Potential Causes of SSA

I came out of homosexuality myself. I understand this condition from the inside out. I have been married for over 35 years. Many reporters have asked me, "Would you love your son or daughter if they were homosexual?" My answer is always the same, "Of course I would, but that would never happen because I know what causes someone to experience same-sex attraction." And yes, all three of my children are heterosexual. My sons are manly and also sensitive. Our daughter is both feminine and powerful.

As a psychotherapist, I have helped hundreds of men and women who experienced unwanted SSA achieve their heterosexual potential and dreams. There is no such thing as a homosexual (noun). There are only people who experience same-sex attraction (adjective) and practice homosexual behaviors—for many different reasons.

The following is a list of ten potential causes that may lead an individual to experience SSA (see the chart at the beginning of this chapter). A combination of experiences and characteristics lead to SSA—never a single factor alone. Parents do not instill SSA in their children. It is the child's perception of their parenting combined with his/her innate temperament, e.g. hypersensitivity, which makes the difference. To see how these factors interact and create SSA in children, please read the case histories of the five celebrities in the next chapter. You may also want to watch wonderful stories of transformation at www.voices-of-change.org.

1. Heredity

- Unresolved family issues
- Misperceptions
- Tendency to feel rejected

"It is assumed [by intergenerational and transgenerational family systems theory] that relational patterns are learned and passed down across the generations and that current individual and family behavior is a result of these patterns" ("Assessment of Intergenerational Family Relationships," *Family of Origin Therapy*, James Bray and Donald Williamson, Rockville, MD, Aspen Publishers, 1987, p. 31).

In family systems therapy, it is well known and accepted that unresolved issues and dysfunctional behaviors of preceding generations are passed down to subsequent family members. At the core of an individual who experiences SSA is a sense of not belonging, not fitting in, and feeling different from others. These thoughts and feelings may be inherited from family members depending upon their circumstances in life, culture, religion, race, and/or ethnicity.

What I and other sexual reorientation therapists have observed is that SSA men and women are highly susceptible to rejection, or perceived rejection, existing for any number of reasons which may stem from generational unresolved issues. Of course, this does not cause same-sex attraction in boys or girls; it is just one contributing factor among many.

2. Temperament

- Hypersensitive
- Artistic nature
- Gender nonconforming behaviors: Male more feminine; female more masculine

As I have mentioned, many or most SSA men and women as children were highly sensitive, or hypersensitive, which led them to react more deeply to the behaviors of their parents, relatives and peers. Often attuned to the emotions of their parents, these children will frequently modify their behaviors to avoid conflict. Other times, they will become pleasers or caretakers. Because of their hypersensitive nature, they may act more passively and therefore be unable to assert themselves in interpersonal relationships. Of course, not all sensitive children will develop SSA.

If the hypersensitive child has an artistic nature, and the parents, relatives or peers are non-supportive of this gift, she or he may experience further rejection. The sensitive and gifted child, in an insensitive and non-support environment, experiences undue stress and anxiety.

A further group of young children, who exhibit what we call "gender non-conforming behaviors," that is, the little boy who acts more effeminate and the little girl who acts more masculine, are particularly at risk for being either ostracized by family members and peers, or these days, encouraged to act upon those tendencies. However, these character traits—(or behavioral phenotypes), the more effeminate boy and more masculine girl—in certain environments are expressed with the purpose of invoking a reparative or healing drive. By that I mean that a child is seeking to successfully bond with his or her same-sex parent, and thus not trying to summon a "gay" identity. When this drive for bonding is achieved, the child will have a healthy attachment with his or her same-sex parent and secure gender identity will ensue.

Therefore, with this understanding, instead of thinking, "Oh, he was born gay," or "She was meant to be a boy," and with deeper insight into the dynamics of the family system, we see an attempt by the birth of this child to heal generational wounds of detachment between either fathers and sons or mothers and daughters. If the father would take the time to join with this effeminate boy, see life through his eyes and experiences, eventually the boy will bond with his dad and internalize his father's sense of masculine identity. The same would hold true for the mother and her more masculine daughter.

Dr. Francis S. Collins, director of the National Institutes for Health and former director of the Human Genome Project, declares that homosexuality is "genetically influenced but not hardwired by DNA, and that whatever genes are involved represent predispositions, not predeterminations" (*The Language of God*, New York, 2006, Free Press, p. 260). With healthy intervention and parenting/mentoring, the child will experience a sense of his or her own gender identity and opposite-sex desires with ensue.

3. Opposite-Gender (Hetero-Emotional) Parental Wounds

- Over attachment to opposite-sex parent (enmeshment)
- Imitation of opposite-sex behaviors
- Abuse: emotional, mental, verbal, physical, sexual

There has been much literature written about boys over-attached to their mothers and girls over-attached to their fathers. Again, this is not a blame game, but naming what took place for the purpose of healing. Drs. Irving Bieber, Charles Socarides, Joseph Nicolosi,

Gerard van den Aardweg, Sigmund Freud, Robert Kronemeyer and many other psychologists and psychiatrists have observed that SSA men have had an abnormally close mother-son attachment. They are inclined to internalize their mother's sense of femininity and become distant and detached from the masculinity represented by their fathers. On the other hand, the daughter may be closer to her father and estranged from her mother, thereby internalizing her father's masculinity and rejecting her mother's femininity. In other cases, the daughter views the mother as weak and/or ineffective, and models her behavior after the more dominant and powerful parent, her father.

Another phenomenon might be the child perceiving that his or her parents wanted a child of the opposite sex. The son therefore acts like a girl, and the daughter acts like a boy in order to please their parents and win their approval and affection.

As mentioned, many SSA women have been abused by men, and not wanting to repeat these unhealthy patterns in relationships, they seek their affectional needs from women.

4. Same-Sex (Homo-Emotional) Parental Wound

- Detachment from same-sex parent
- Neglect: lack of intimacy
- Abuse: emotional, mental, verbal, physical, sexual

Lack of sufficient bonding between the son and his father and daughter and her mother is often at the core of anyone who experiences SSA (homo-emotional wound). Again, the perception of the child becomes her or his reality. Oftentimes, these hypersensitive children perceive rejection from their same-sex parent based on character differences, i.e., an authoritative same-sex parent and a hypersensitive child. The mismatch in character between father and son or mother and daughter often creates the sense of detachment in the pre-SSA child. Without the parent perceiving these cues, the daughter or son becomes susceptible to further rejection by same-sex peers. The stage is then set for the potential development of same-sex attraction and same-sex erotic feelings during or after puberty. Those desires represent a means to achieve bonding that never took place in the earliest years of child development.

5. Sibling Wounds / Family Dynamics

- Name calling
- Same-sex siblings/relative's rejection
- Abuse: emotional, mental, verbal, sexual, physical

Yet another variable that may contribute to the development of feeling outside of one's gender—not fitting in, and being different—is insufficient bonding with siblings or relatives of the same sex, boys with brothers and male relatives, or girls with sisters and female relatives. These sensitive children are often people-pleasers, trying to keep everyone happy at the expense of their own needs. How many parents have said, "My son was the perfect little boy." Well, boys generally by nature are more assertive and mischievous, and not so sweet. Be careful of the "good little boys," encourage them to be themselves and not please everyone else.

Some SSA women had poor relationships with their sisters, and/or were mocked and teased by men in their family. This leaves a deep wound in their hearts, not fitting in with their same-sex peers and relatives, and feeling hurt by men. Some SSA boys grew up in families of all girls and women, and some SSA girls grew up in families of all men. These factors may also contribute to gender identity issues.

6. Body Image Wounds

- Late bloomer
- Shorter/taller – skinner/larger
- Physical disability

Late bloomer, early maturation, physical disabilities, shorter, taller, skinnier, or larger—these are some characteristics that may result in body-image wounds for the pre-SSA boy or girl. A hyper-sensitive boy who experienced insufficient bonding with his father and over-attachment with his mother, now incurs more self-esteem issues by being different from other guys, i.e. too tall, too thin, too short, too large, not athletically inclined. The result is a profound sense of gender inadequacy, feeling on the outside looking in. If they were late bloomers, they often felt different and alienated from their peers. The pre-SSA girl may experience similar thoughts and feelings based upon her perception of her body image and the opinions of her parents, relatives and peers.

7. Sexual Abuse

- Homosexual imprinting
- Learned and reinforced behaviors
- Substitute for affection and love

Sexual abuse may be another contributing factor to the development of same-sex attraction; however, it is never the sole cause. The pre-SSA child is more susceptible to sexual abuse because of his or her lack of attachment to same-sex parent and/or peers. Sex then becomes a substitute or replacement for emotional and relational intimacy with others of the same sex. If the behavior is repeated over time, it may create a neurological basis for the further development of same-sex attraction in the male or female. Again, this is just another contributing factor and not a prerequisite to experience SSA. In my therapy practice, and the counseling practice of my colleagues, approximately 50% of our clients experienced some form of childhood sexual abuse.

There is usually a difference between SSA men and women when it comes to sexual abuse. Many boys who carry father and/or male peer wounds were easy targets for male sexual abuse, because they were longing for that connection with their dads and other guys. Many girls who develop SSA were sexually abused by men. They may seek female affection to soothe their wounds and protect themselves from further abuse by men.

8. Same-Sex (Homo-Social) Peer Wounds

- Name calling / put-down
- Teacher's pet
- Non-athletic boy / more athletic girl

Both SSA men and women often experienced a tremendous sense of emotional wounding because of same-sex peer rejection—guys didn't fit in with the other guys, and girls didn't fit in with the other girls. Often they were called names such as "sissy," "faggot," "queer," "pansy," "dyke," "tomboy." Many SSA boys hung out with the girls, and SSA girls hung out with the guys. While SSA boys were not athletically inclined and received teasing and taunting from their male peers, some SSA girls were more athletic, and if detached from their female peers, may have been ostracized as well. Then, during or after adolescence, those normal needs for same-sex peer bonding became sexualized.

Another source of wounding for the pre-SSA child is boys mocking girls ("You're so butch," "You're a dyke") and girls mocking boys

("You're such a faggot," "You're so sweet and girlie"). Not only do they receive put-downs from their same-sex peers, but opposite sex peers as well.

9. Cultural Wounds

- Promotion of the homosexual myth—born "gay" and cannot change
- Cultural abuse: media, Internet, educational system, and politics affirm and promote homosexuality
- Pornography

After a boy or girl experiences wounding or lack of attachment with their same-sex parent and/or peers, or incurs any of the other factors previously mentioned, then same-sex attractions develop during or after adolescence leading to homo-erotic feelings and desires. The world then mistakenly says, "You're gay," or "You're lesbian." As we have learned, this is a false paradigm leading hurt children down the road to homosexuality under false pretenses. Also, with behaviors from performers in the music and entertainment world, it is becoming trendy to experiment sexually or act bisexually.

Many kids are being raised in single-parent families, often lacking the attention and affection of the same-sex parent. This leaves him or her vulnerable to being enrolled into the false "gay" paradigm, whereby their normal needs for bonding will become eroticized by members of the same sex. The media, educational system and the entertainment industry, driven by the homosexual myth, have created a false identity called "gay." But there is no such thing as a "gay." There are only hurt children looking for love in ways that will not fulfill their deepest desires for real love.

Again we go back to the Homosexual Manifesto and the false indoctrination of our youth and our culture into the innate, immutable paradigm. If boys or girls experience SSA in adolescence, we immediately label them as "gay," rather than understand there are specific causes that led him or her to experience SSA. No one is essentially born this way. There are always reasons why anyone develops homosexual feelings. (Remember, some kids experiment with same-sex friends at the onset of adolescence, but this does not make them "gay" or SSA.)

10. Other Factors

- Divorce
- Death
- Adoption
- Religion
- Spiritual factors

There are any number of other life experiences that may contribute towards the development of SSA and low self-worth in a sensitive boy or girl. If the parents divorce, the people-pleasing child may blame himself or herself. If a parent dies, the child may perceive it as personal rejection and abandonment. When a struggling child hears "hell and damnation" or homosexuality is an "abomination" from the pulpit of his or her place of worship, further feelings of guilt and shame burden this sensitive child (read the story of Kevin Jennings in the next chapter).

If the child was adopted, she or he may feel rejected from their birth parents and never securely attach to the adopted parents (read Greg Louganis's story in the next chapter). This sense of rejection may reside deep in the unconscious, creating a pattern of insecurity.

Note: Many people with a strong faith background believe there might be spiritual influences that drive homosexual feelings in boys or girls and men or women. Even if there is validity to this, it is imperative to realize that when the other ten potential factors are addressed, healing occurs and change will ensue. By strictly viewing SSA as a "spiritual problem," one will not fully heal and fulfill their innate heterosexual potential. As psychotherapist Jan Frank stated, "You cannot heal a spirit, or deliver a wound."

> "For a homosexual adaptation to occur, in our time and cul-
> ture, these factors must combine to (1) create an impaired
> gender-identity [feeling of masculinity or femininity], (2)
> create a fear of intimate contact with members of the oppo-
> site sex, and (3) provide opportunities for sexual release with
> members of the same sex" (Dr. Judd Marmor, as quoted in
> *Growing Up Straight*, Peter and Barbara Wyden, New York:
> Stein and Day, 1968, p. 18).

A combination of any of these ten factors may lead an individual to experience SSA: (1) Heredity, (2) Temperament, (3) Hetero-emotional wounds, (4) Homo-emotional wounds, (5) Sibling wounds and family dynamics, (6) Body-image wounds, (7) Sexual abuse, (8) Social and peer wounds, (9) Cultural wounds, and (10) Other factors. *The severity of wounding in each category will have a direct impact upon the amount of time and effort it will take to heal.*

Please read other books for greater details about the potential causes of SSA and the process of healing (see a list of resources at the back of this book).

> *No one is essentially born with SSA.*
>
> *No one chooses to experience SSA.*
>
> *The only decision is to live a homosexual life or resolve unwanted SSA.*

Let me make it perfectly clear: I am not saying that people who decide to live a homosexual life are wrong. I respect them and the path that they have chosen. For me, I chose a different path, the road less traveled, and, as Robert Frost has written, that has made all the difference. What I wish to convey is that people are not essentially born with SSA, and that change is possible for those who pursue this option. The fact that there are underlying causes of homosexual feelings and there exists the potential for change is *not* widely publicized. There has existed for decades a heavily financed media mechanism, which would have us believe the opposite.

Seven Stages of "Coming Out"

To better understand the heart and mind of those who experience SSA, I would now like to share with you the seven stages of the "coming out" process. The following descriptions come from my book *Gay Children, Straight Parents* (pp. 18-22):

Stage 1 – Causes of SSA

Stage 2 – Same-sex attractions begin

Stage 3 – Conflict over SSA

Stage 4 – Need for belonging

Stage 5 – Indoctrination

Stage 6 – Identity acceptance as gay, lesbian, bisexual, or transgender

Stage 7 – "Coming out" process

Stage 1: Causes of SSA. We just mentioned the many contributing factors that result in homosexual desires such as disrupted attachment between father and son or mother and daughter (this may be the child's perception, not the parent's failure), over-attachment to the opposite-sex parent, hypersensitivity, lack of bonding with same-sex peers, sibling wounds, cultural wounds, name-calling, sexual abuse and body image wounds. Again, it is never one thing alone that causes SSA but a combination of factors.

Stage 2: Same-sex attractions begin. SSA begins at various ages for different people depending on several factors: the child's temperament, physiology and perceptions; family history at particular times; and social or cultural events. Most often, the eroticization of another person of the same sex begins around ten to thirteen years of age, near the onset of puberty. In some cases the desires may occur sooner, if a child has undergone sexual abuse or some other significant trauma (e.g. early exposure to sex). For others, homosexual desires may emerge later on, in the late teens or early twenties, or in some cases during a mid-life crisis. More and more married men and women are "coming out" and often times disclosing their long battle with SSA. Such people repressed their same-sex attractions for many years, hoping and praying they would disappear.

Stage 3: Conflict over SSA. The young struggler may ask himself, "Why do I have these feelings? What would others think of me if they knew I had homosexual desires?" A child may wonder, "Is it a sin to feel this way? Does God still love me?" Most often, these boys and girls experience tremendous feelings of pain, confusion, guilt, shame, and loneliness. These emotions are exacerbated when the young person is unable or unwilling to talk freely with family and friends. Other times, she or he may be involved in a strong religious community, and to disclose about her or his SSA is too scary for fear of being rejected or judged.

Kids today easily find "answers" outside their immediate circle of loved ones and spiritual community. They access pro-homosexual information on the Internet or attend a Gay Straight Alliance (GSA) meeting in middle and high school or a LGBT club in college. The new addition to the LGBT nomenclature is "Q" meaning "Questioning" youth, so that people who have a fleeting attraction for someone of the same sex may be led to believe that they too are "gay," hence, LGBTQ.

As mentioned, some young children experiment with members of their own sex while entering into adolescence. Others have had sexual encounters while intoxicated, and others while attending boarding school. This does not make these young people same-sex attracted or "gay." This is situational behavior and the majority of these people move on to develop strictly heterosexual desires.

Stage 4: Need for belonging. The struggle continues: "I don't fit in. I don't belong. I'm not like the other kids." During puberty, what were once emotional desires for bonding with the same-sex parent and/or same-sex peers now become sexually inflamed yearnings. The emotional need for connection becomes eroticized. However intense the desire may feel, it is important to remember that the basis for all SSA is conflicted emotional needs and lack of sufficient gender identity, not sexual attraction.

Stage 5: Indoctrination. As we see in the world today, any young person who experiences the least amount of same-sex attraction is told, "You were born gay. You cannot change. Efforts to change are harmful." These youngsters have to work very hard to accept themselves as "gay" or "lesbian." This process generates conflicting thoughts and feelings. I believe that those who experience SSA initially know, in their conscience, that homosexual behavior is out of sync with natural law. Nonetheless, they are inundated with the idea that SSA is genetically or biologically determined—they're born that way, therefore, they cannot change.

The "born gay" myth is much like the old folk tale *The Emperor's New Clothes*. In this story, an emperor is fooled into believing skilled craftsmen are creating beautiful clothes for him. In fact, two charlatans create nothing. Going along with the hoax, the emperor parades through the city streets wearing nothing. Not wanting to appear foolish, all his subjects exclaim, "What a wonderful set of new clothes!" Then a child stands up and says, "The emperor is naked!" At that moment the emperor realizes he has been duped. "We should all be like this child and speak the truth," he proclaims.

So it is today. Most of us have been deceived, even though we instinctively know that humans are heterosexually designed: a man and a woman fit together perfectly and naturally, two men or two women do not.

Stage 6: Identity acceptance as gay, lesbian, bisexual or transgender. At this juncture, strugglers come to terms with their SSA and adopt a "gay," "lesbian," "bisexual," or "transgender" identity. They have anesthetized their conscience through social indoctrination and finally self-acceptance. Hearing the homosexual myth repeated often enough, with little or no debate, establishes it as "fact." At this stage, you and the rest of the "homophobic" society may be perceived as the enemy. (A phobia is an irrational fear of something, not a principled disagreement. "Gay" activists have misused this term.) "You don't understand. You don't know what it's like to be gay and be on the outside looking in." The Us-vs.-Them complex is reinforced.

Stage 7: "Coming out" process. Often parents are the last to know about a child's SSA, not because they are the least important, but because they are the most important. Gender-confused young people are especially sensitive and fearful of rejection, so they first "come out" to their friends or siblings who seem a bit safer. They are developing a support system fearing that mom and/or dad may reject them. Finally, he may share with his parents, "Please accept me for who I am. I'm your gay child. God made me this way!" Or she may angrily exclaim, "If you refuse to accept me just the way I am, you're homophobic and unloving." The truth is, they are afraid to lose their parents' love.

What if you find it difficult to accept a family member or friend's homosexual identity and/or life? How do you love them without endorsing something you may not believe in? This will be the subject in Chapter Five. The path of "coming out" is most often lonely and painful, frequently walked alone. Today, strugglers get support from LGBT groups on-line or at their local Gay Straight Alliance in school. The sad thing is that young people are totally unaware that there are alternatives to living a homosexual life.

Coming Out Straight *Is* Possible

> Dr. Robert Sptizer, professor of psychiatry at Columbia University, stated, "Like most psychiatrists, I thought that homosexual behavior could only be resisted, and that no one could really change their sexual orientation. I now believe that to be false. *Some people can and do change"* (*Archives of Sexual Behavior*, October 2003, Vol. 32, No. 5, pp. 403-417).

Over the past twenty-five years as a psychotherapist, I have had the privilege of assisting those who experience unwanted SSA achieve their heterosexual dreams through therapy, healing seminars, and teleconferencing classes. I know personally and professionally that *Change Is Possible!* My life is a testament to this fact, as are the lives of thousands of other men and women worldwide who have come out of homosexuality. Since people are not essentially born with SSA, the opportunity for transformation is available for those who seek change (watch powerful testimonies: www.voices-of-change.org).

Keys to healing unwanted same-sex attraction are: (1) discovering the root causes of SSA—the hidden meaning behind the desires, (2) healing wounds of the past—one must feel in order to heal, (3) gaining support from others, and (4) experiencing the love of God. Same-sex attracted men need the support of heterosexual men, and SSA women need the support of heterosexual women. Personal motivation is important if someone wants to change. In Chapter Five, I will share practical suggestions how to help those who are "gay" identified fulfill their true gender identity.

It is also important for someone seeking to resolve unwanted SSA to find effective counseling. I mention "effective" counseling because most therapists have no idea how to assist those who experience unwanted SSA. Since 1973, there has been little or no training of therapists in the field of sexual reorientation therapy (also known as reparative therapy, gender affirming processes, or pejoratively called "conversion therapy"). The National Association for the Research and Therapy of Homosexuality (NARTH) is the first therapeutic organization dedicated to assisting those with unwanted SSA (www.narth. com). Membership to NARTH consists of therapists, educators, and concerned citizens. You may contact NARTH for a referral therapist in your area or country. Be aware that some of those therapists may be sympathetic to this issue; however, they may not have specific training in this field. I have developed a Counselor Training Program to equip professional therapists and ministry leaders how to assist those who experience unwanted SSA and their loved ones. You may find information about this program at www.pathinfo.org.

Interview candidates if you seek a therapist. You may ask them the following questions: (1) what is your education and training in the field of sexual reorientation therapy, reparative therapy, or gender-affirming therapy?; (2) How long have you worked in this field and what is your success rate?; (3) What therapeutic approaches do you use in helping people heal? (Please read Chapters Four and Six in *Coming Out Straight* to better understand the healing process and therapeutic modalities.); (4) Do you really believe that people can change?; and (5) Do you believe in God (if this is important to you)? The individual seeking help is going to be sharing very deeply and entrusting the therapist with guiding him or her on this journey of healing. It is essential that you understand the therapist's education, training, success rate, therapeutic approaches, and perspective on this controversial issue. Set up a free 15-20 minute in-person, telephone, or Skype consultation before making a commitment to enter therapy.

Marriage is *never* the solution for SSA. Why? Because a woman can never meet the homo-emotional/homo-social love needs of a man, and man can never meet the homo-emotional/homo-social love needs of a woman. In the process of healing, first a SSA man must heal with other men, and a SSA woman must heal with other women. I was told, "Find the right woman and she'll straighten you out." Well, I did, and she didn't. Not because she couldn't, but because there were so many wounds in my heart and soul that needed to be healed. Like every other SSA man, I needed to first securely bond with healthy, heterosexual men in order to experience my own manliness before being successful as a husband and father. I made all the mistakes possible, thereby becoming an excellent therapist and coach for those seeking change! And I'm not the only one. Thousands of men and women worldwide have changed and fulfilled their heterosexual potential. As Winston Churchill declared, *"Never give up!"* SSA is a message from the soul trying to teach the individual about himself or herself.

With these principles in mind, I hope you'll enjoy reading the story of Christian.

Christian's Story

It was July 1995 and I had come to the end of a very long, long road. I was gay—a homosexual. It was time to give up the charade I had been playing for forty-four years. It was a deep, dark secret I had hidden from everyone. This feeling of gayness had been a part of every aspect of my life, and I could no longer tolerate the incredible pain. I supposedly had it all. I had a great job and social life. I had the suburban lifestyle. I had a beautiful, devoted, loving wife of over twenty years and the greatest daughter and son a father could ever hope for. Ultimately, however, I always felt trapped as a homosexual pretending to be a straight man in a straight world where I just didn't belong. It was time to come out as a gay man.

I grew up as a kid in the 1950s and went to college in the late '60s. I was not part of the pre-"coming out" acceptance of gays in the 1970s. As a child, teenager, and college student, there was no one available in the public sector to openly go to for support. "Queers" and "fags" was the terminology I knew, and I certainly felt I fit the mold. It was always too frightening as a kid and young adult to actually admit I was a queer. I thought if I just play the part of a straight man, maybe it would all go away. The general public did not accept gayness; it was definitely taboo.

With the 1970s a flood of information came to me from strong, openly gay men and women. The media blitz and the changing world was letting me know that, "Hey, you're gay, and it's okay." It was not okay with me. I had already married and started a family. I ached to be a part of the gay scene, but I also ached for my sexual feelings to just go away. I was upset with and jealous of gay men because I felt alone, isolated, and detached from any identification with heterosexual or homosexual men.

Up to the early 1980s, I had only once gone to a Christian counselor about my "depression." He informed me I was a latent homosexual, probably should break off my engagement and look at nude pictures of women to get the "cure." Needless to say, I dismissed his advice and pretended this counseling had never occurred.

By the early1980s, I was like a volcano ready to explode. I had never had a sexual encounter with a man. I had lots of fantasies and wet dreams, but never actual physical encounters. Theater had been a way for me to be around and near gay men. It was after a theatrical performance I confessed to a friend, who was gay, that I had sexual feelings for men. Soon after this confession, I got invited to his apartment where he introduced me to homosexual sex. It was like thirty years of dead, suppressed weight lifted from me. I soon found another cast member who was more than willing to engage in sex with the new gay on the block. I thought I was in heaven, but it quickly turned to hell for me. I felt empty, alone, frightened, deceitful, guilty, dirty, and ultimately, heading in a direction where I did not want to go.

I was living a double life. I confessed to my wife I was gay. She did not accept this as truth. She knew I was not gay, but her ability to help me was just not there. A straight psychologist tried to help me, but he had no clue what to do. He knew I wanted to stay married, but did not know how to help me. I read some literature and got the idea that this was genetic and that was that. To help support the genetic theory, my sister had confessed to the family that she was gay! I dropped the psychologist, and my wife and I pretended that the problem went away. I hated myself.

A few years after this, in the mid 1980s, I had again stayed away from gay sexual encounters. However, my wife's and my sexual life was in shambles. I hated sex with my wife. This was not the best criterion for wedded bliss. She sent me off to a New Age encounter with some guru who could "zap" the homosexuality out of me. I was desperate and scared, so I agreed to go. It was horrific. I question if this man was possessed by some demon that really wanted to suck out my soul. He worked by intimidating and humiliating me in front of hundreds of his followers. He pronounced that I was the devil and for his followers to shun and stay away from me. I fled this scene and was sure any hope of ridding myself of gayness was totally unrealistic. I again began to periodically engage in sexual encounters with men. It became both an addiction and a short-lived fix. I could go months without having sex with a man, but then if something happened in my life that was stressful, I would flee for a homosexual encounter. I kept searching for the perfect man, and I somehow believed that if I found him, he would be strong enough and love me enough to take me away from the straight world. I would then be safe, warm, and loved. As the years passed, I realized that this was a fantasy that just wasn't coming true.

So, I take you back to July 1995. My anxiety level was about to explode. With deep regret, I had secretly begun to see a counselor for gays to transition out of my marriage to the gay community. I felt thoroughly depressed, but felt I had *no other choice* for the sake of my wife and for my survival. At the same time, my wife presented me with a book written by Richard Cohen. She had seen Richard on a TV show many months before. She had diligently tracked down this book. On this TV show, Richard claimed he could transition men from homosexuality to heterosexuality. I was furious and skeptical. I decided no more wacko gurus for me. It was garbage. My wife then gave me the best ultimatum of my life: "Go see Richard, or move out and get a divorce." I loved her enough to try one more time, but felt it was another hopeless course.

I was totally and utterly skeptical of therapy that gave me a choice to be straight. I was too old at forty-four to change. There could be no magical "hocus-pocus." I had my feet firmly planted in the genetic theory. My childhood encounters and my parents had nothing to do with this gayness that I felt. Richard Cohen's therapy *would not work*.

I wish there were a way to convey true gut feelings. It was a dark, broken individual who had his first therapy session with Richard. For me, building a trusting relationship with him was the key that began to open the door of healing for me. Being able to pour out my true feelings to someone who was really listening was an important first step for me. He had walked the walk, so I could accept what was truth for him. His living example gave me the initial prospect that healing just might be possible. I knew I wanted to transition, so I would take it one day at a time.

I began to learn that there were major key factors that contributed to my homo-emotional feelings. It was important for me to learn that my same-sex attractions were the sum of these key factors. My childhood, in my eyes, had been perfect. My parents had provided me with a beautiful home, clothes, food, and social and travel experiences. An incredible realization was that neither of my parents was demonstrative in physical touch or verbal affirmations. I have no memory of either of my parents ever telling me they loved me. I have only one memory of my mom hugging me. My father never hugged me. I realized how devastating this was for me. I had no healthy touch experience from my parents within my childhood memories to the present. I clearly remember fantasizing, as a young child, about my dad's friends holding me and having sexual fantasies about them. I was not getting healthy touch from anyone.

I believed that the only time one touched was for sex, so I would dread any touch by anyone, as it would lead to sex. Mentoring sessions, where healthy men and women held me safely, brought incredible healing and my biggest breakthrough. I felt like a little child being loved by a parent in a very healthy way. I discovered quickly that I *could* get healthy touch. I knew I had been seeking touch with men in an unhealthy way. I'd just wanted to experience affection and had used sex to get it.

Memory work of the inner child was also another key factor in my transitioning. When Richard asked me to draw pictures with my non-dominant hand and write down feelings and experiences, I truly thought this was a crazy and a stupid task. However, I quickly had clear memories of childhood. It came out on paper about how I left myself wide open for inappropriate touch by one relative and sexual abuse by teenage boys who would baby-sit and take me on outings. This helped to peel away more layers of what had felt like, "I'm gay."

Group therapy sessions, with people who were working towards healing, were incredibly supportive. It was another key to my healing to have a support network and individuals with whom I could say whatever I needed to say. Sometimes it was to tell them how I was healing or to tell them I was having a bad time and felt like acting out. It could be to tell them I had sexual feelings for another person in the group, and to discuss why those feelings were there and how to resolve them in a healthy way.

My pastor is a great friend and very secure in his heterosexuality. We get together to talk about anything and everything. He is a great mentor. We go to the gym, play tennis, get together for lunch, and just hang out. I am totally comfortable with our friendship.

Massage therapy really helped me to accept appropriate touch. Having deep pressure applied to my muscles felt as if my body was transitioning from a sexual touch to the acceptance of normal, healthy touch.

In July 1995, I started a therapy course that changed my life. I had individual therapy, sometimes twice a week, for a little less than two years. I was in a support group for the same amount of time. At the end of this time, it became apparent that I was living a wonderful, productive life with my wife, children, and friends. I had and have the tools necessary to continue to grow as the man I have become. My darkness and anxiety are completely gone. I really enjoy sex with my wife. I no longer have sex attractions for men. I am not, nor ever was, gay. I had addictive homo-emotional feelings for men. I feel fantastic because I had a choice made available to me. I believe strongly that I had to make a choice for *me*, and it was a choice I believe in. I chose to transition, and *transition is possible*.

I no longer identify with the man I was before July 1995. That was a lifetime ago. I feel reborn. At the beginning of my therapy, I felt so alone. A friend in my support group said, "If you think you're alone, then you are wrong. You are not alone anymore." I have God, my wife, my two children, and the great prospects of what life holds for me each day!

Conclusion

Here are some of the causes of Christian's SSA:

1. There was insufficient bonding between Christian and his father, therefore he was unable to incorporate his dad's masculinity and feel his own maleness. As Christian mentioned, he never recalled being held or touched by his dad. This created a deep wound in his soul and need for male affection and attention.

2. There was some connection with his mother, but not as much as he needed. This increased his desire for physical affection, which was later to be used and confused through sexual abuse.

3. Christian's temperament was highly sensitive in a relatively insensitive environment. His needs went unmet and unnoticed.

4. Christian recalled numerous experiences of child sexual abuse by men and boys in the neighborhood. This created a pattern of sexualizing his need for paternal and fraternal intimacy. From that time, Christian used sex to obtain some form of male affection.

5. Like many people in their forties, unresolved issues of the past begin to manifest during this stage of life, often called a "mid-life crisis." Our shadow, unconscious or unresolved parts manifest in present-day life through unwanted desires or behaviors. Christian, though married to his loving wife, would act out sexually with other men. This was a means whereby his wounded self, those unconscious issues repressed for many years, worked to get Christian's attention in order to resolve his past.

Suggestions

How family and friends can help men like Christian:

1. I can't say it often enough: Fathers, *please* bond with your sons by showing them your affection, attention and concern. Mothers, *please* bond with your daughters by displaying appropriate physical affection, and participate in their activities. Dad's join in your son's world, and mom's be engaged in your daughter's world. Grandfathers and uncles bless the lives of your grandsons and nephews. Grandmothers and aunts bless the lives of your granddaughters and nieces.

2. Christian learned to sexualize his need for male affection and attention after being sexually abused as a child. In the process

of healing, it was imperative for him to experience closeness with heterosexual men who were not interested in any form of sexual activity. This was a great healing for Christian. Three healthy, heterosexual men stood in the gap for me as well, helping me heal the many years that I learned to sexualize the legitimate need for healthy male bonding.

3. Mentor someone like Christian, who never experienced healthy paternal/fraternal affection. If an adult had offered this to him as a child, he never would have had to sexualize that desire. Men, reach out to those who experience SSA, let them know that you care, whether or not they wish to live a homosexual life or seek change. Women, reach out to women who experience SSA, and show them healthy feminine love, sans the sex. What their heart of hearts is calling out for is acceptance and healthy affection. Men, be a brother, a friend, a mentor. Women, be a sister, a friend, a mentor. In the process, you will change someone's life. I promise too, knowing such a beautiful man or woman will enrich your life.

CHAPTER THREE

Clues Why Five Celebrities Experience SSA

Why We Believe They Experience SSA

	Lack of Bonding with Same-Gender Parent	Over-Attached to/ or Wounded by Opposite-Gender Parent	Adoption or Death of a Parent	Sibling Wounds	Sexual Abuse	Body-Image Wounds	Same-Gender Peer Wounds	Hyper-Sensitivity	Socialization Into "Gay" Mythology
Greg Louganis: Olympic diver	✓	✓	✓			✓	✓	✓	✓
Melissa Etheridge: Singer/Songwriter	✓	✓		✓		✓	✓	✓	✓
John Amaechi: Retired NBA player	✓	✓				✓	✓	✓	✓
Rosie O'Donnell: Comedienne, actress	✓	✓	✓		✓	✓		✓	✓
Kevin Jennings: Founder of GLSEN	✓	✓	✓	✓		✓	✓	✓	✓

All these men and women have similar causes for their SSA, further demonstrating that same-sex attraction is an acquired condition.

© Richard Cohen, M.A., 2010

LGBT activists fought long and hard to redefine SSA as "gay." Why? Because the word "gay" means happy. Remember, someone who adopts a "gay" identity has accepted the "born this way and cannot change" myth, while others who experience unwanted SSA do not take on such an identity. With the socialization of the "gay" paradigm, homosexuality becomes legitimized and public opinion is changed. This makes it possible for prejudice and rejection to turn into love and acceptance. As we learned in the seven stages of "coming out," many men and women who experience SSA adopted a "gay" identity in order to experience some semblance of self-worth and pride after feeling like outcasts for much of their lives. We have also learned that no one is essentially born with SSA, but everywhere we turn we hear: "I was born gay, it's who I am. I've felt this way since I was a child." Oprah and other celebrities continue to affirm homosexuality without ever looking behind the curtain to see what's there.

In this chapter, let us look at the background of five celebrities who define themselves as "gay" or "lesbian." I have summarized their similarities in this chart. As we consider their experiences and family dynamics, I think you will notice some familiar patterns emerging:

- **No one is essentially born with SSA**

- **No one simply chooses to have SSA**

- **Change is possible**

Throughout each of these evaluations, a summary of the celebrity's life experiences appears in italics, interwoven with my own perspective, analysis and comments. I would have preferred to incorporate more direct quotes from each author; however, most of their publishers were not forthcoming with permission. Therefore, I have used their words sparingly. Direct quotes appear inside quotation marks and are not in italics.

Greg Louganis

Greg Louganis is one of the most celebrated divers of our time, with four gold medals at the Olympics, six time World Champion, and 47 National Championship titles. He also experiences SSA and is living with AIDS. Mr. Louganis is a brave, persistent and extremely sensitive man. He developed homosexual feelings through no fault of his own. As you will see in this evaluation, it is apparent how Greg's SSA developed. Throughout his life, as detailed in his autobiography Breaking the Surface, *he battled with depression and low self-worth.* All quotes are taken from his book (page numbers are in parenthesis).

Dr. Joseph Nicolosi, a leading psychologist in the field of sexual reorientation therapy, describes the triadic relationship of a sensitive boy detached from his father, and over-attached to his mother. Greg fits this profile to a tee. In Greg's own words, you may observe the many causes of his SSA that were identified in Chapter Two. All of these early experiences resulted in substance abuse, same-sex attraction, and abusive homosexual relationships.

"What you will read here is the story of a lonely boy who struggled with dyslexia and discrimination, yet discovered he had a great gift for acrobatics and diving. It's about a shy kid who battled low self-esteem, bouts of depression, and conflicts over his sexuality yet still went on to become one of the most accomplished divers of all time" (*Breaking the Surface*, Greg Louganis with Eric Marcus, Sourcebooks, Naperville, IL, 2006, pp. viii-ix).

Throughout Greg's autobiography, we observe the many risk factors of his SSA:

1 – Hypersensitive temperament and low self-worth

2 – Detachment from his abusive father

3 – Over-attachment to his mother

4 – Abuse by male peers

5 – Body-image wounds

6 – Adoption

HYPERSENSITIVE TEMPERAMENT / LOW SELF-WORTH

Greg was hypersensitive. He never felt strong enough to stand up for himself, and therefore internalized all the negative messages he received from within and outside of himself. Greg felt rejected by his biological parents, adopted father and male peers. Depression was a major issue throughout his life. He attempted suicide three times. His self-worth was always tied to his diving. We call this performance-based behavior, whereby one tries to gain acceptance and love through one's activities and achievements.

Acrobatics and diving provided relief from his difficult childhood. He questioned if his adopted parents really loved him; meanwhile the kids at school were beating him up. He felt so hopeless.

Greg experienced dyslexia from an early age and was put into a special education class, as his teachers didn't understand his learning disability. From 12 years of age, he was miserable, felt isolated from the other kids, and hated his physical appearance. His self-perception was "terrible." He believed that no one could understand him, a common experience for many young children with SSA. Throughout his formative years, Greg "played negative messages" over and over again in his head—no one wanted him, no one really cared about him, and he was deeply flawed. Greg was also called "sissy," "fag," and other hurtful names by kids at school. It made him feel "worthless," like he had no right to live. Being so shy and withdrawn, he didn't feel worthy of acceptance by his peers, so he used diving to attain self-worth.

DETACHMENT FROM HIS ABUSIVE DAD

Greg's relationship with his father was fractured. He developed a defensive detachment (an emotional wall of separation) toward his dad at a very young age. His father was authoritative, stoic, unaffectionate, and an alcoholic. Greg's deep homo-emotional wound laid the groundwork for his future same-sex attraction.

Greg became close to his father during the latter years of his life, when his dad was diagnosed with cancer. Even though their relationship improved, the devastating wounds of Greg's childhood were not healed.

"Mom said that Dad was born an angry man. Dad wasn't the type of father who would give you a hug and say that he loved you. He was stoic and, except for anger, not very good at expressing his emotions" (28). *The family walked around "on eggshells," not to upset their dad or he would become very upset while drinking. This was the norm in the Louganis household. By the time Greg was twelve or thirteen years old, they would simply sit in silence during dinner. He sometimes ran away from home when his Dad drank and threatened to beat him.*

Greg's father didn't like his dancing and acrobatics, and did not attend any of his performances. Because the kids at school were constantly labeling him "sissy" and "faggot," Greg internalized the same negative messages from his father. On the other hand, his dad was over involved with Greg's diving activities. Greg thought his father's involvement in his diving was more about him than about Greg.

OVER-ATTACHMENT TO HIS MOTHER

Greg's maternal grandfather was an alcoholic, just like his dad. Greg's mom was unable to have children, so they adopted Despina two years before they adopted Greg. As with many SSA men, Greg was extremely close to his mother and quite distant from his father. Being a hypersensitive boy, he more easily connected to women. Throughout Greg's life, he continued his very special and close relationship with his mother, typical of most SSA men.

Fathers pay attention! When you have a sensitive and gifted son, be sure to join in his world and then bring him into yours. As I described in Chapter Two, the first critical bonding time that is essential for the healthy development of a boy's sense of masculinity, is from the ages of 1½ to 3 years old. During this period of time the boy learns to walk and talk. He then needs to separate from his mother and identify with his own gender role model, his dad, or a substitute father figure. If this doesn't happen, then the boy will continue to gender identify with his mother.

Some researchers and therapists believe this factor is one reason there are more SSA men than SSA women, because girls, even though they too will differentiate and individuate from their mothers, will continue to gender identify with her. The boys have this extra developmental task— separating from mom and bonding with dad—which is why fathers are so important for their sons during this and other developmental stages. The good news for dads of SSA sons is that you can restore the relationship with your adolescent or adult son at anytime (of course, the same holds true for moms with SSA daughters). It is never too late to heal! (Please read Gay Children, Straight Parents: A Plan for Family Healing *for the "how to's" of reconnecting to your SSA children.)*

Greg's mom made all his costumes for acrobatics and attended all his performances, unlike his dad who stayed away entirely. She was also supportive of his diving and didn't pressure him, only wanting Greg to be happy.

"If Dad got mad, she usually just shut up. She said she didn't want to give him any excuse to do anything. Mom learned from being with her dad that you don't talk back to a drunk. That's how she learned to keep the peace. Unfortunately, that's how I learned, too" (30).

ABUSE BY MALE PEERS

Greg was passive in relationships with tough boys. He learned this pattern of behavior from his mother, his primary role model and source of love. From her, he learned to keep his mouth shut, to keep the peace at all costs. This cost Greg dearly, especially in the relationship later on with Tom, his abusive partner of six years.

When Greg was ten, he was in a very bad fight. A kid punched him and slammed his head into the asphalt until he bled. His father witnessed the entire episode without intervening. "He might as well have been the one throwing the punches. That he would be there and not help me was so terrible that I blocked it from my memory. All I remembered was the fight itself and feeling that my father thought I deserved what I got" (36).

Greg didn't know how to stand up for himself, as his father never taught him how to do so. Greg also had a distorted view of himself and others because of being disconnected from his father, male peers, and ultimately, himself. Greg used his diving to gain affection, attention, and affirmation from others—again, performance-based behavior—seeking love and approval through his achievements.

It bears repeating that this never works because children need to be loved for who they are, not for what they do. Adults who use their talents and abilities to gain acceptance are often internally troubled, avoiding their core pain and wounds.

Home life was horrific for Greg, and so was school. He found no refuge anywhere except through acrobatics and diving. From the very first day of elementary school, the kids called him names because of his dark, Samoan complexion. Then came the derogatory comments, "faggot," "sissy," and more. Unfortunately, when Greg went to his teacher for support, she did nothing. This led Greg to believe that something was wrong with him.

From third grade on, Greg got beat up a lot, especially by the rough kids at the bus stop and in the school cafeteria. He would tell them he didn't want to fight, or, "I know you can kick my ass, so why bother?" Then they would call me a 'sissy-boy faggot'" (34).

Greg had no close friends at school, and never had a "best friend." He was constantly being beaten up, and even the girls cheered the bullies on. Greg internalized all these experiences, thinking that the kids were right and he was wrong, and that he somehow deserved to be treated abusively.

BODY-IMAGE WOUNDS

Greg was detached from his physical appearance, which is common among same-sex attracted individuals. Once someone detaches from their primary gender role model, in this case Greg's father, and once he detaches from his same-sex peers, then he rejects his own sense of masculinity, gender identity, and physical appearance, as if to say, "I don't want to be like dad or the other guys." He then spends the rest of his life looking for that unattained self-acceptance and love in the arms of other SSA men. However, it never works very well because both are looking for the same thing, and it's something that neither one of them will experience: the fullness of their own masculinity and gender identity. As you will soon learn, this is quite evident in the lives of Melissa Etheridge, Rosie O'Donnell, John Amaechi, Kevin Jennings and most SSA men and women.

Greg became known as a sex icon after his first Olympics, but internally he still felt like an outcast. People continued to shower Greg with compliments about his handsome appearance; however, due to low self-esteem he couldn't receive any flattering remarks.

ADOPTION

Adoption was yet another source of rejection for this highly sensitive boy. The core belief of feeling abandoned was a great source of pain throughout Greg's life—rejected by his biological parents, by his adopted father, and by his male peers.

The first nine months of his life, Greg lived with a foster family. His biological father was Samoan and his biological mother was a blond-haired, blue-eyed Northern European, like his adoptive mother. Eventually Greg accepted the love of his adopted parents in spite of the trauma he experienced with them. "But the emotional damage had already been done, and I've struggled throughout my life with trusting whether anyone genuinely cared for me" (43).

SUBSTANCE ABUSE

While in school, Greg smoked cigarettes and marijuana, used other drugs, and drank alcohol to anesthetize his pain. Eventually he stopped smoking and drinking, but he continued to use pills until he began therapy in his thirties.

Greg started smoking "pot" to fit in with the smart kids at school because he always felt that he didn't measure up to their intellectual prowess. Greg drank a six-pack of beer each day for many years.

SUBSTITUTE DADS (DIVING COACHES)

John Anders was Greg's second coach. Greg envied John's sons because he wanted an emotionally warm and available father like John. Mr. Anders spent time with his kids, something Greg's father never did, and thus Greg always felt like a "bother" to his dad. Through his relationship with Mr. Anders, for the first time in his life, Greg felt cared for by a male authority figure.

In January of 1976, Greg moved in with his third coach, Dr. Lee. Although Greg "loved" Mrs. Lee, he transferred onto Dr. Lee similar feelings and responses he had for his own father, perceiving Dr. Lee as "stoic," "stern" and "cold." He wished Dr. Lee had been more like John Anders, who was the "fantasy father" of Greg's dreams.

Greg grew very close with Mrs. Lee, once again typical behavior for many SSA boys—close to female authority figures, distant and detached from male figures. They feel more comfortable in the world of women and detached from the world of men. Mr. Lee's harsh character served to make Greg further withdraw into himself.

Greg's next and final coach, Ron O'Brien, was more like John Anders. He helped Greg feel more secure, building up his sense of self-worth. "He was more nurturing…" (89). *Greg found out in 1987 that he was HIV positive. He shared this with Coach O'Brien, who was very loving and supportive. Greg had to take medication every four hours. Ron said,* "We'll get through this together" (178). *However, despite Ron's positive support of Greg, he still harbored the pain experienced from his dad and male peers. Time doesn't heal all wounds. They only fester until we deal with them.*

HOMOSEXUAL RELATIONSHIPS

Greg experienced a conflict in his soul. I believe that every person who experiences SSA initially goes through this stage. Everyone's conscience knows that sexual relationships between those of the same sex are inherently incongruent with natural law. Because Greg never successfully connected and bonded with his dad and same-sex peers, he longed to be loved by men. This is a natural desire of every child. Those core love needs must be met in the critical years of child development; otherwise he will look for love through sexual relationships. What were once legitimate needs for male bonding then becomes eroticized after adolescence. Greg wanted to be held and feel safe, which he never experienced with his father or male peers. If only he had received the right kind of support and love from men who understood the meaning of his SSA, he would never have had to experience so much heartache and pain in abusive homosexual relationships.

Greg had a crush on Soviet diver at his first Olympics in 1976. This man held and caressed him, and Greg said that he "wanted to stay" in his arms forever…the longing of a child for his father's love. As far as Greg shared in his book, there was no real sexual relationship between the two of them, just cuddling and being close. Greg recalled being attracted to men from the time he was 7-8 years old. He was confused about these attractions, but after being held by this diver, he longed to be held again by a man.

When Greg was 16, he had his first sexual experience was with a man who was in his thirties. Greg enjoyed the sex while it occurred, but felt guilty afterwards. He just wanted to be physically close and "held." At that time in his life, Greg believed that sex between two men was sinful, according to his faith.

Greg had three short-term boyfriends followed by a six-year relationship with Tom, and then a four-year relationship with Steven. His first boyfriend was Daniel. It was a very unhealthy and co-dependent relationship. Next was Jeff, who had sexual relations with women throughout their relationship. His third boyfriend was Kevin. They got into arguments and physical altercations, beating on each other. Greg transferred his tremendous need for love and acceptance onto his male partners, that which he did not experience from his dad or male peers. This creates an emotional time warp, re-enacting the father-son relationship, trying to get a man to love him. However, the core issue is his need for male bonding and acceptance.

Greg began dating Tom in 1982. They moved in together after the 1984 Olympics. They were together for six years.

As Harville Hendrix states in his book, Getting the Love You Want *(Henry Holt and Company, New York, 2008), "Each of us enters adulthood harboring unresolved childhood issues with our parents, whether or not we know it or will admit it. Those needs have to be met, because their satisfaction is equated, in our unconscious minds, with survival. Therefore, their satisfaction becomes the agenda in adult love relationships" (p. 26).*

Tom was taller than Greg, had "broad shoulders" and a "good-size" chest" and was five years older (Greg was 22 when they started dating). Greg's memories of his time with Tom were "too painful to recall," and that he is "embarrassed" by what he let Tom do to him during their six years together.

Tom was quite logical, like Greg's dad, as well as eloquent, always in charge. He did almost everything for Greg, making him feel totally cared for: "This was my fantasy: to be loved and taken care of. And I loved Tom all the more because he showered me with so much attention" (134). *Again, Greg is like a little boy searching for his father's love and acceptance in the arms of his boyfriend. He thought he had struck gold in finding Tom, but in reality he was partnered with another abusive father figure.*

Before they moved in together, Greg dated other men. When Tom found out, he went crazy, demanding that Greg call each of the men he had seen, and tell them he was sorry and couldn't see them again. Greg felt humiliated, and once again, like the boys who beat him up, Greg felt responsible, that everything was his fault (even though he and Tom were not in an exclusive relationship when he dated those men). Following the phone calls, Tom became "enraged," took a large kitchen knife, grabbed Greg's neck and raped him. Simultaneously, he berated Greg using disgusting words. Greg cried and begged Tom to stop. Tom told Greg that he deserved this. After everything was over, it was Greg who apologized for hurting Tom! This was not the only time that Tom would prove to be violent in their relationship.

Tom told Greg that he wasn't getting big endorsements because he was too feminine…more put-downs. It made Greg doubt himself and feel guilty, even though he was supporting both of them. Tom's rules according to Greg: Don't ever bother him when he's on the phone; he has to win all games; Greg serves him all his meals; he controls all of Greg's schedule; he showed almost no affection after living together; and Greg couldn't ask questions about his late night outings. Years later, Greg found out that all through their relationship, as Tom accused Greg of being unfaithful, Tom was a prostitute, hustling on Santa Monica Boulevard! Can you imagine how shocked and shameful Greg felt when he learned of this?

As you can see, Tom was treating Greg in the same manner that Greg's father treated his mother. And he reacted to Tom in similar ways his mother reacted to his father. He was re-living the dynamics of his parent's relationship. His inner child, so desperate for his father's love, was trying to change the abuser Tom, who represented his dad. This never works, as Greg eventually discovered. "All I really wanted from Tom was for him to love me and to show me affection, but he was never the kind of man you would describe as loving or affectionate" (159). *Eventually, Greg stood up to Tom and asked him to move out. Tom threatened Greg with blackmail, to reveal his homosexuality to the press and speak slanderous things about him. Finally, they reached a settlement where Greg would support him for the rest of his life (as Tom was living with AIDS by that time). Tom remained abusive toward Greg until the end. He passed away in 1989, the same year Greg's father died! Greg then met Steven. They were together for four years before splitting up. Greg is still living with AIDS.*

CONCLUSION

Perhaps now you can better understand the life of Olympic gold medalist Greg Louganis. It is amazing what he has been through. He practiced diving five to six hours daily, year after year, while internally suffering. The greatest pain in my heart about Greg is that he should never have suffered like this. Greg's child-like need for male affection could have been satisfied in healthy, non-sexual relationships with heterosexual men.

Following are suggestions for Greg and SSA men like him:

1. *Instead of sex, Greg needed male mentors to help heal his father wounds. Ron was a wonderful coach for Greg; however, Greg needed to grieve the many losses of his past. Like most children of alcoholics, Greg didn't openly express his feelings and needs to Ron and others while growing up. If you see a young boy whose father has rejected him, put your arm around him, show him healthy masculine love, and allow him to grieve the many losses he has experienced in his life.*

   When I was presenting the basic causes of SSA at a conference many years ago, the soundman approached me after the talk. He stated, "You just described my life. However, my baseball coach literally put his arm around me and became the dad I never had. Without him, I know that I would have ended up developing homosexual feelings. He saved my life!"

2. *The unspoken rule in the alcoholic family system is that no one is allowed to have their own thoughts, feelings, or needs. Greg's mother, the enabler or codependent, did her best to keep the peace, and to keep the children from upsetting dad. One reason Greg threw himself into aerobics and then diving was to medicate his pain. Eventually he began to drink and use drugs to further anesthetize his wounds. Greg needed to get in touch with himself and heal his wounds; however he used sex to obtain some male affection and attention, which he never experienced from his father or male peers.*

   When you see a child stuck in an alcoholic family system, do your best to suggest that the entire family seek help. Greg's mother followed the pattern of her mother. Greg followed his mother's pattern. The chain needed to be broken. Outside intervention is often necessary in this type of situation.

3. *If you see such a sensitive boy in school, on the swim team, any-where in your community, please stop others from teasing him. Bullying is wrong all of the time, regardless of the child's nature. No one stood up for Greg, not his own father, none of the kids at school, or any teachers or administrators. Stand up and stop the bullying! Greg and others like him deserve to be treated with respect.*

4. *Boys who are too close to their mothers and distant or detached from their fathers need someone to intercede. SSA can be pre-vented. If you see a relative or close friend in this situation, gently speak to the parents. Parents love their kids, but sometimes they need a gentle nudge from an observer to help set love in order.*

Melissa Etheridge

"What I really am is this little girl looking for acceptance. Looking for love and trying to fill up this hole inside of me that has always been empty" (*The Truth Is ... My Life in Love and Music*, Melissa Etheridge with Laura Morton, Random House, New York, 2002, p. xiv). "I was tortured by my need for love and affection—my need to find someone who could fill up the emptiness inside me. I'm still driven by that need as a songwriter" (31).

Melissa Etheridge is beautifully transparent in her autobiography The Truth Is ... My Life in Love and Music. *I deeply admire her passion, authenticity, and vulnerability, baring her soul throughout this tell-all autobiography. She recalls childhood experiences in Kansas, beginning with a painful birth, a cold and disapproving mother, the sexual and physical abuse of her older sister, rejection by same-sex peers, and finding acceptance only through her father. Within Melissa's family there was no expression of emotion; it was a cold and unsafe place for her as a child and adolescent. She was born on her older sister Jennifer's birthday, which created a lifetime of rivalry for attention and for what little affection was available within their family. Jennifer, who was four years older than Melissa, sexually and physically abused her from the time she was 6 through age 11, instilling within Melissa a psychological and neurological pattern of intimacy with women which involved sexual behavior. Music became Melissa's refuge, a safe place of comfort and solace. Her dad supported her pursuit of music and her SSA, while her mother was disapproving of both. Unable to bond or identify with her mother, Melissa modeled herself after her only real source of love, her father. Throughout Melissa's life, she sought refuge in the arms of many abusive and unavailable women, who were similar to her mom and Jennifer. This type of behavior is characteristic of many SSA women, transferring onto their partners a child's need for acceptance and love.*

I believe that Melissa Etheridge may experience SSA because of the following factors:

1 – Insufficient mother-daughter bonding

2 – Over identification with her father

3 – Sexual and physical abuse by her older sister

4 – Abusive same-sex relationships

5 – Gender dis-identification: feeling more masculine than feminine

MOTHER WOUND

Melissa's birth, on May 29, 1961, in Leavenworth, Kansas, was terribly painful. Her mother went into labor at home. When they got to the hospital, the doctor was on break, so the nurses held Melissa in for 15 minutes. Her birth experience felt crushing to Melissa, as she was born "black-and-blue and bruised." Her family never spoke about this, or any other important matters of the heart. Melissa felt that she was physically and symbolically bruised from the time of her birth.

Melissa's mother did not communicate with her; they had quite a distant relationship. On the other hand, Melissa loved her grandmother who lived in Arkansas. It was the only positive and nurturing female relationship she had during her formative years. Melissa felt appreciated, accepted, and loved by her grandmother, but not by her mother. She felt unconditional love for the first time in her life. Melissa's grandmother died when she was in the sixth grade, and typical of her family, there was no expression of emotion or grief, even at the funeral. After this loss, Melissa shut down emotionally and expressed her feelings through her music.

When her mother found out about Melissa's homosexuality, she was typically cold and rejecting. She wrote her daughter a letter telling of her disapproval, which deeply hurt Melissa. They never discussed it again. As an adult, Melissa never felt accepted by her mother. Melissa experienced a profound wounding in her heart and she never sufficiently bonded with her mother, who should have been her primary role model of femininity. As we'll see, she spent many years of her life moving from one relationship to the other, seeking to obtain the femininity she never internalized, and a mother's love and acceptance never felt.

OVER IDENTIFICATION WITH FATHER AND MASCULINITY

Melissa's father was supportive of her music. Her dad bought her first guitar, drove her to band practice and performances. She was much closer to her father than her mother, which is typical for many SSA women. Melissa internalized his masculinity, being more identified with him and dis-identified with her mom and the femininity that she represented. "I was very much a tomboy, completely awkward in my body. My mother never showed me how to do my hair, how to dress 'right.'" (6).

Melissa's appearance seems to be more masculine than feminine, as she modeled herself after her father, who was her primary source of love during the formative years of her life. When she revealed her homosexuality to her father, he was completely accepting and supportive, unlike her mom who was both rejecting and judgmental. "My whole life I'd wanted to be like my dad" (126).

SIBLING WOUND / SEXUAL ABUSE

From the time Melissa was six years old, Jennifer began to systematically and repeatedly sexually and physically abuse her. Jennifer would first speak sweetly to Melissa, and then give her directions how to "touch" her...inappropriately. Afterwards Melissa felt both horrible and shameful. Following the family code, there was never any discussion or sharing about what transpired. As this continued, Melissa began to disconnect, or disassociate from her body, just being an "observer" to what transpired. This phenomenon is called "psychic splitting," common among those who experience sexual abuse. The individual feels too much pain, and detaches from her body. Some may even feel that they rise above their bodies when being abused, observing what is taking place, because the pain is just too great to contain.

Jennifer became increasingly manipulative and angrier toward Melissa as she grew, tormenting her with acts of abuse and violence, like slapping across the face for no apparent reason. Randomly, she would scream and frighten her. Two of Jennifer's behaviors—manipulation and controlling—are traits that Melissa says she finds attractive in women, especially ones she is romantically involved with. Dr. Harville Hendix, again in his book Getting the Love You Want, *calls this the unconscious marriage, being attracted to someone who carries the negative characteristics of our caregivers/siblings, and then trying to change the person in order to obtain the love so desperately wanted and needed as a child.*

After the physical and sexual abuse ended when Melissa was 11 and Jennifer 15, Melissa began to eat in order to numb the feelings of emptiness and pain. She tried to fill the "hole" inside with food, movies, and music. It was the only time that she felt safe and comforted, escaping into the world of make believe and "fairy tales." This is typical behavior of children who experience abuse, a defensive reaction to dull the pain, to medicate themselves, not knowing how to reconcile the contradictions in their lives.

ABUSIVE SAME-SEX RELATIONSHIPS

Melissa was needy because of the coldness she experienced from her mother and sexual and physical abuse by her sister. While growing up, Melissa found no one to share with about her heartaches and pain. In her sophomore year of high school, she became intimate with Jane, who began to act like Jennifer, slapping Melissa across the face for no reason. A cycle of intimacy and abuse became a repetitive pattern in many of Melissa's adult relationships with women.

"I'm trying to get from other people what they are simply not capable of giving to me. Wanting it. Needing it. Craving it. Obsessing over it. But never attaching the concept of ever receiving it" (34). *Melissa was well-known for her "one-night stands," sleeping around with many women. She would seduce them, win them over, and then leave them. This was her addictive relationship pattern for many years. Melissa enjoyed the feeling of conquest, but she always withheld herself from them.*

Melissa went from one relationship to the next, attempting to fill the emptiness in her heart and resolve the painful relationships with her mother and sister. It never worked. She kept drawing to herself women who were emotionally unavailable, one after another. Then she met and moved in with Julie, actor Lou Diamond Phillips ex-wife, and they had two children. For a while they became poster women for the homosexual community, appearing on the cover of Newsweek *and interviewed by* 20/20. *Over the years, their relationship became increasingly strained for numerous reasons and eventually they broke up.*

"She [Julie] so represented my mother to me—that same distant and aloof attitude … I just felt so left out, so lost and confused"

(140). One of Melissa's most popular songs, "Come To My Window," is about her emotional pain regarding Julie. After twelve years together, Julie decided that she was not a lesbian, announcing, "I'm not gay!" Melissa was devastated. This type of behavior is common among some SSA women. Their sexuality seems to be more fluid, with some reverting back to heterosexuality.

In April 2003, Melissa was engaged to actress Tammy Michaels. They "married" in Malibu, CA in September 2003. Their wedding was featured on ABC's InStyle Celebrity Weddings. In October 2006, Tammy had twins, a boy and a girl. In April 2010, Melissa and Tammy broke up. These types of relationship often fail to work out because both partners are looking for the same thing, which neither one of them has experienced: a successful bond with their mothers and a secure sense of their own feminine gender identity.

CONCLUSION

> "This was supposed to be the time of my life. I had made it as a rock star. I had a big house, a fancy sports car, and a relationship that was a lot of work. I guess I expected all of that to fill the big, dark, empty black hole in my heart … I thought that when I became a famous rock star, all of my problems would fade away. That's why I wanted to be famous in the first place: to solve my problems. I thought that being loved and adored by millions of people would surely fill up that deep, endless pit I carry inside myself. I thought that I wouldn't be starved for that attention, affection, or redemption if I had the love of millions. But I was. I was still emotionally malnourished" (182-183).

This reveals Melissa's "truth" about her life. Just as Greg Louganis had done, Melissa used performance-based behaviors in an attempt to fill the "empty black hole" in her heart. She used her rock star status, her relationships with women, and the many accolades she's received over the years. None of these things worked.

This is the pain of so many men and women who experience SSA. They are looking for unattained love in the arms of other men or women—desperately seeking to fill their need for parental and peer bonding. Melissa never experienced the nurturing touch and care of her mom, was repeatedly sexually and physically abused by her older sister, and was attached to her only source of love and acceptance in the family, her dad, who became her gender role model. It is easy to observe why Melissa Etheridge developed SSA, and how it continues to play out in her life.

Here are some suggestions for healing that can help Melissa and other women with similar issues:

1. *Melissa needed a warm, maternal mother's love, affection, and support. If Melissa had come to know other warm-hearted women like her grandmother, who would have doted on her, showed her the ways of women, taught her how to dress, helped her do her hair, taken her out, and most of all simply loved her for who she was, she would have had a very different life.*

2. *Melissa was drawn to abusive relationships with women, mirroring Jennifer and her mother's treatment. Some women who experienced sexual abuse, and who didn't sufficiently bond with their same-sex parent, learned to substitute sex for intimacy. Melissa needed healthy female peers to embrace her, demonstrating healthy feminine love.*

   If you are a heterosexual woman, and you know another woman who experiences SSA and was sexually abused, chances are she didn't bond successfully with her mother and/or same-sex peers. Please stand in the gap for her. Wrap your arms around her. If she comes on to you, she's just doing what she was taught to do as a child. Hold her hands and look into her eyes and gently say, "I love you and I don't need that from you." What a new message of hope and acceptance she will receive, a gift of love never experienced before in her life!

3. *Melissa Etheridge and Rosie O'Donnell, as well as many other SSA men and women, go from relationship to relationship. They are seeking that unattained parental and peer love. If you have experienced love from your parents and/or other mentors in your life, then please be the giver of the gift of love to a SSA man or woman. Women like Melissa need your love and affection. You can become the solution to the homosexual dilemma!*

John Amaechi

Former NBA player John Amaechi is another example of how a boy may develop SSA, as described in his autobiography Man in the Middle *(ESPN Books, New York City, 2007), and in an interview from* The Advocate *(a homosexual magazine). John lacked positive male role models while growing up. His father left the family when John was just a little boy. He, his mother, and two sisters fled from Boston, MA to Manchester, England in order to escape his father's abusive threats. John's dad followed them with repeated attempts to kidnap his children. Meanwhile, John's maternal grandfather was verbally abusive and critical of John throughout his childhood.*

John's "Mum" acted as mother and father, his source of love and protection, his primary role model. His maternal Grandmother was another source of healthy feminine love. John was also close to his two sisters. But from his male peers in school, John experienced rejection, name-calling, and incessant mockery for his physical appearance and lack of athletic prowess. As a young boy, John was overweight and non-athletic. He ate to numb his pain, and was called a "whale" by the other boys in swim class. Like other SSA men, John was a hypersensitive boy. He was quite introverted and preferred to spend his quiet time alone reading. It was in these solitary times that he found solace. His "Mum" worked very hard, managing two jobs, caring for others through her medical practice.

In my estimation, John Amaechi's SSA is a result of:

1 – Profound father wound

2 – Persistently abusive grandfather

3 – Over attachment to mother

4 – Hypersensitive temperament

5 – Body-image wounds

6 – Male peer wounds

John experienced father, grandfather, and male peer rejection, excessive female attention, and a hypersensitive temperament. Due to these factors, he was unable to navigate his way in the world of men. From the age of 17, as a 6' 8" teenager living in England, John was discovered by a basketball scout. Through intense practice and excellent coaching, for the first time in his life, John began to gain a feeling of being valued. Finally, he felt a sense of belonging and acceptance amongst his male peers. Basketball increased John's self-esteem. Until then, he had been a fatherless, "overweight," sensitive, non-athletic "misfit" and "nerd." Unfortunately, John never dealt with the core wounds that created his SSA, never reconciling his father, grandfather, and male peer wounds. This became more apparent when reading John's account of his relationships with men in the NBA, how awkward and ill at ease he was with the other players. To this day, John does not like his body and keeps his shirt on while in the presence of others. This is the direct result of internalizing all the derogatory names he heard while in gym and swim class.

Like Greg Louganis and Melissa Etheridge, John Amaechi used his basketball talent as a performance-based behavior to gain acceptance and love. As we've seen, this never works because the "inner child" doesn't want to be accepted for what he does, but for who he is. John received lots of attention for his basketball talent, but still the little boy within seeks the unattained paternal and fraternal love. When sex enters into this equation through homosexual relationships, it prevents the child within from experiencing unconditional love.

In my opinion, John's SSA grew from the aforementioned experiences, as well as his inborn temperament of hypersensitivity. Because the world does not understand the true meaning of SSA, John was led to believe that he was born "gay." John is an intelligent, sensitive, and insightful man. He was never offered correct information about why he experienced homosexual desires. John is a man of great character, values and tenacity. His mother, "Mum," as he called her, instilled within him a tremendous work ethic and respect for all human life. As a medical doctor, she was an excellent role model, giving of herself for the sake of others. John gained her deep sense of public service, offering his free time while in the NBA to mentor at risk teenage boys.

Someday, I would like to sit down with John and share ideas, opinions, and thoughts. He is presently working on a degree in child psychology, while mentoring young children in England, having already established several athletic centers. He is also an inspirational speaker, traveling throughout England and the USA, sharing about his "Plan," how he made it to the top, and also sharing about his life as a "gay" man in the NBA. He is also a spokesperson for the Human Rights Campaign, mentoring other gender confused boys and girls. If such a man truly understood the real facts about SSA, what a powerful force he would be to help future generations heal and fulfill their true gender identity. Oprah promoted John on her show, and now John promotes "gay" rights. (I am grateful to John's publisher for giving me permission to use his quotes liberally.)

PROFOUND FATHER WOUND

John was born in Boston and, at four years old his family moved to Manchester, England to escape his abusive father.

"I should have been overcome with fear about my disgraced father's threats to hunt us down and make us disappear, the fear of losing a comfortably middle-class existence for a new life in faraway land..." (6). "My father, it turned out, became emotionally abusive to his wife" (9). *John's dad left a pile of unpaid bills for his wife to pay. He then returned to his native country of Nigeria. When he returned to the USA,* "Mum made it clear he was no longer part of our family" (9). "As his menacing behavior and his veiled contempt escalated, Mum decided it was time to flee to Manchester" (9).

"My father had sent Granddad a letter threatening to kidnap us and spirit us away to Nigeria, never to be seen again. We knew it was no idle threat, because he did show up now and again, and Mum would sequester us at a friend's place while he stayed in the UK" (11). "When Dad came to the UK, Mum would somehow learn of his whereabouts. We would be driven to the safe house of one of Mum's friends. Our nights away were scary because we knew Mum would be confronting our dad. When Dad finally stopped showing up, I was nearly 10. Only then were we allowed to take our bikes around the block, temporarily out of Mum's watchful eye" (11).

John lived with his Mum, two sisters, grandmother and cruel grandfather; there was no healthy male role model in John's childhood. Significantly, as an adult, when his father died, John had no desire to attend the funeral.

PERSISTENTLY ABUSIVE GRANDFATHER

Besides having a threatening, abandoning father, John's grandfather was also abusive and critical. The lack of a warm and encouraging male figure in John's life created a vacuous hole in his soul. This male mentoring wound and lack of salient paternal love helped to lay the groundwork for John's future SSA.

"Granddad cast a shadow of fear over us. We weren't a bad lot, but he had a knack for making us feel like the worst kids in the world when Grandma wasn't around to keep him in check. As a male role model, something my childhood lacked, he left a lot to be desired. Perhaps his attitude helped me better understand the kids whom I would eventually mentor. Without the warmth from Mum and Grandma to temper Harold's coldness, I might have ended up as furious as he was. Coupled with the bullying I experienced at school and a father who threatened to kidnap us, I understand the reason for my utter disdain for sadistic coaches" (254).

OVER ATTACHMENT TO MOTHER

John's Mum became a medical doctor in Scotland. There she met her future husband Jon Amaechi who was from Nigeria. They traveled to Nigeria to assist others during the Biafran War. Next they moved to Boston and married. John's mother worked at Mass General Hospital and his dad started a manufacturing business. John was born on November 26, 1970. Muriel was born one year later and Uki a year after that. In Manchester, John's Mum worked day and night to support her three children. Eventually she became a partner in a surgical practice. As you read John's words, his role model was his "Mum," as there was no man to show him the ways of men.

"I knew Mum would never allow me and my younger sisters, Muriel and Uki, to come to harm. Through sheer force of will, she surrounded us with a comforting blanket of security" (6). "Mum is the person who was my role model...From her I learned perseverance despite great odds, courage in the face of danger, and stoicism against evil" (7). "Mum tried to protect us from the ugliness of those early days by maintaining a steely silence, so there's much her kids don't know (7). "It was inspiring just watching her take on the world, and the determination she demonstrated rubbed off. Her children have never been afraid of setting goals and letting nothing stop us in the pursuit of them" (12). "What I most hoped to emulate was Mum's bedside manner, her ability to serve as an emotional as well as a medical caretaker, to soothe the hurt, no matter how dire...I still swell with pride when someone stops me on the street in England—not to recognize me as the former NBA player, but to regale me with glowing stories about how Mum touched their lives" (12).

Mum was John's hero, caretaker, protector and mentor. His father was, in his and his mother's eyes, a failure, abusive, and a threat to the family. This was a sensitive boy deeply connected to his mother and completely cut off from and fearful of his role models of masculinity, his dad and grandfather. Robert Bly, in his book Iron John, *details how a boy cannot grow into manhood without the active participation of healthy male figures.* "A mother's protection, no matter how well intentioned, will not do as a substitute for the father's protection" *(Robert Bly, Iron John, Vintage Books, New York, 1990, 67). Bly also speaks about the phenomena in which a boy is protected by his mother, and thereby learns to feel as a woman, losing his own sense of gender strength and connection to the masculine.* "Jung said something disturbing about this complication. He said that when the son is introduced primarily by the mother to feeling, he will learn the female attitude toward masculinity and take a female view of his own father and of his own masculinity" *(Bly, 24). Furthermore he states,* "If the son learns feeling primarily from the mother, then he will probably see his own masculinity from the feminine point of view as well" *(Bly, 25). As loving and protective as John's Mum was, it disrupted his psychosexual development as a male.*

HYPERSENSTIVE TEMPERAMENT / BODY-IMAGE WOUNDS / MALE PEER WOUNDING

John hated his body. Being a hypersensitive boy, he was unable to stand up to the bullies and set them straight. John's childhood lacked a protective, salient dad or positive male role model to show him the ways of men. No boy can become a man without the investment of positive male role models. Robert Moore states, "If you're a young man and you're not being admired by an older man, you're being hurt." *There was no father around to help strengthen and affirm John's masculinity.*

"By age 10, near the end of primary school, I already stood a head above my classmates at nearly six feet tall. In fact, I was taller than many of my teachers…Not only was I tall; I was brown-skinned and increasingly round…I stood out not so much like a sore thumb but a fat one" (13). "Especially in gym. Donning my first uniform— bright red shorts—belly protruding, was an exercise in humiliation, worse even than Granddad's signature haircut. Team photos were posted on the public notice board, enshrining my shame for the entire school" (14).

John experienced humiliation in his swim class for being overweight: One classmate yelled, "He's supposed to be able to hold his breath: he's a whale!" "It was one of those moments when you swear you can feel a part of yourself die inside. I'd been christened a monster forever. I dunked my head to avoid the rising ridicule. Whenever I showed up for mandatory swim, I'd be greeted with similar name-calling. And it wasn't just one bully. It seemed everyone joined in the fun. All I could do was force out a pretend laugh, but deep down I had to admit the words cut…The experience in the swim class had lasting psychological ramifications. For my entire adolescence I wouldn't get near a public pool without covering my entire body the instant I emerged from the water. Even today I'm rarely spotted anywhere near a body of water." (15). "At any rate, my self-consciousness about my body made me want to avoid sports of any kind" (16).

"I despised exertion of any kind. I hated to sweat. The more strenuous the exercise, the more I loathed it. Even long walks sent me around the bend. To this day, I've never understood those who enjoy the supposed 'high' of intense workouts. To me it is pointless pain and suffering. I've experienced plenty of endorphin surges after an intense workout, but I must say I've had better highs from a cup of Earl Grey tea. Instead, I came up with a far superior activity to pass the time: sitting in a chair reading and drinking enough delicious tea to fill a swimming pool" (17).

John retreated into the world of books. One reason was to avoid social criticism and seek solace in the world of make believe, magic, and fantasy. No one could hurt him there. You can see the parallel in John's life with that of Melissa, who sought refuge in movies and music, and Greg, escaping the trauma of his life through diving.

"I read and reread every volume in the Hardy Boys series. It never bothered me that every story was identical, save for the setting…It's no surprise my taste ran to the escapist. There were no social pressures or demands, no put-downs directed at me, and it was always others who felt the sting of hurtful words. Like a lot of kids, I identified with outcasts who took on great magical powers to overcome their evil tormentors…The massive amount of time I spent with my nose buried in books helps explain why I had few friends" (17). "Mum threw me a 10th birthday party. Only one kid showed up" (18).

Books and food became substitutes for healthy male friendships, paternal love and affection. There is a book entitled, When Food is Love. *The author explains that many people use food as a substitute for real love in their lives. John used his studies and food to fill those vacuous spaces in his heart and soul.*

"Where athletics failed me, academics made me. I may have been physically loathsome, but with enough reading I figured at least I could be more clever than everyone else. It was my last hope to be exceptional at something, anything, to become an intellectual super-hero" (21).

John studied for tests night and day and still didn't make the top grades he expected. "Fat and dumb. Over and over, I berated myself before bursting into tears" (21). "Along with books, food was my greatest diversion. On the way to Stockport Grammar School, I'd stop at the sweet shop and fill my pockets with Bon Bons, Pear Droops, Cola Bottles, Gummy Bears, Twix, and Kit Kats. Not sur-prisingly, I ballooned further. The bigger I got, the more I needed my candy therapy. My candy stash did have one advantage: I would offer sweets to kids I hoped to befriend as a sort of bribe. It worked. My 11th birthday party was packed with kids of all sorts" (18).

John's words ring with the same frequency as those of Greg Louganis. Self-deprecation, self-loathing, and low self-esteem were common expe-riences of both boys. Because neither Greg nor John bonded with their primary role model of masculinity and other buddies at school, they also rejected their own masculine bodies, a common experience of SSA men.

"Public showering was and is not high on my list of favorite activities. I preferred to head to my next period, sweat pouring off my clothing and onto the classroom floor, to the humiliation of undress-ing in public" (24). "What I enjoyed was not so much the sport of it [basketball], but the sense of accomplishment and the accolades, which came from every direction with even the slightest hint of improvement" (28). "As a teenager with low self-esteem, basketball had given me a life, but it had also denied me one" (158).

Until John started to play basketball, he lacked any sense of self-worth. He detested his body, disliked sports, and felt different from the other boys. Name-calling was part of his social life at school. Detached from his father and grandfather, detached from the other guys at school, he was also disconnected from his own body and sense of masculinity. This of course, in my opinion, led to confusion about his sexuality and the development of SSA through adolescence.

CONFUSION ABOUT HIS SEXUALITY AND GENDER IDENTITY

"The Plan" John refers to below was what he created with his Mum in order to maintain his integrity while pursuing his goal of being a professional basketball player. He first noticed attractions to the other boys in the high school shower room. Now in college, he began to experiment sexually. He kissed a volleyball team player in the men's locker room at Penn State.

"For days I could still taste the salty sweetness of his tongue, which seemed to have an almost chemical charge when it touched mine. I kept returning so these encounters must have done something for me, fulfilling a nascent longing to be touched, recognized, deemed attractive. They were some confusing combination of fervent, sordid, disquieting, and thrilling all at the same time. That they were not part of The Plan—in fact, they were contrary to it, and that made them even more alluring" (111).

"The pro locker room was the most flamboyant place I'd ever been this side of a swanky club full of martini-drinking gay men. The guys flaunted their perfect bodies. They bragged of their sexual exploits. They checked out each other's cocks. They primped in front of the mirror, applying cologne and hair gel by the bucketful. Some guys just lacked self-consciousness. Others clearly liked to show off. I can't blame them: If I had three percent body fat, I'd probably flaunt it too. They tried on each other's $10,000 suits and shoes, admired each other's diamond studded rings and necklaces. It was an intense kind of camaraderie that to them felt completely natural, but was a little too close for my comfort. I stood in the corner in baggy clothing or wrapped in an oversized towel, dreading having to reveal my body on the walk to the showers. As I surveyed the room, I couldn't help chuckling to myself: And I'm the gay one. Hah" (140). "Coming out threatens to expose the homoerotic components of what they prefer to think of as simply male bonding" (141).

These comments reveal a significant gender wounding in John's psyche and soul. Men learn to be men by hanging out with the guys. In healthy child development, first a boy bonds with his Dad, or a positive male role model. Next, in the homo-social stages of bonding—between the ages of nine to twelve or thirteen—boys bond with other boys. From this, he obtains a healthy sense of his own gender prowess, being one of the guys, a man among men. John missed all of this, revealed by his perception about men joking around, checking each other out, and showing off their strong bodies. All this is viewed through the lens of one who is ashamed of his body and insecure about his masculinity. Being comfortable about his masculinity and his body is not part of John's experience. Because he was not taught to understand the true meaning of his SSA, John eventually "came out" to his close friends and family, and began to engage in sexual relationships with other SSA active men.

CONCLUSION

When John began to play basketball at 17 years old, he finally experienced healthy male mentoring in the form of basketball coaches. At last some wonderful men devoted their time and attention to him. But unfortunately, the emotional damage from his childhood was already lodged in his soul. And then the cultural paradigm finished the job: "You are born gay and that's that." As with Greg Louganis and Melissa Etheridge, John used his talent to gain love and acceptance, which, nonetheless, didn't heal his broken heart. He had already constructed an emotional barrier, not wanting to be hurt once again by men. After puberty, those legitimate needs for male bonding and connection became sexualized. Until his childhood wounds are grieved and reconciled, no amount of homosexual relations will heal the broken and needy child within John.

As you can see from John's own words, he is a very bright, caring and sensitive man. If he had been given the correct information, the outcome would have been entirely different. Still today, if John would endeavor healing his past wounds by dealing with the initial causes of his SSA, he would be able to fulfill his true gender identity and naturally come into the fullness of his innate heterosexuality.

John entered the NBA: from the Cleveland Cavaliers, to pro teams in Greece, Italy, England, France, back to the NBA with Orlando Magic, Utah Jazz, Houston Rockets, and finally the New York Knicks (but he never played for them). He made the best of each situation. During those years, he mentored over twenty young teenage boys, and became the legal guardian for two of them—giving to them all what he himself never experienced. It breaks my heart that John, and so many others like him, would be living a different and more fulfilling life today if they had been taught the truth about SSA and experienced healthy love from heterosexual men.

Following are some suggestions for healing that would be helpful for John and other men who wrestle with similar issues:

1. *John needs male mentors to help break through his defensive detachment, walls protecting his heart that he constructed as a young boy to keep from being hurt by his dad and grandfather. John is comfortable in two roles: (1) mentoring boys, and (2) engaging in homosexual relations. Both keep him "safe," but miss the mark to heal the wounded child within.*

John desperately needed healthy male mentors in his formative years of life. Without a father, and constantly enduring criticism by his grandfather, John never internalized his own sense of masculinity. By joining with someone of the same gender through homosexual relations, his psyche is attempting to fulfill unattained paternal and fraternal love. Dr. Elizabeth Moberly describes this as a "reparative" drive, whereby the individual seeks to bond with men because of unattained love in childhood. In this way he is attempting to incorporate that which is lacking within him, mainly a deficit of masculinity. Sex can never heal those primal needs for love and gender identity.

2. *If an uncle or male friends of the family had stepped up to the plate in John's youth, spent time with him, and showed him the ways of men, this most likely would have prevented John from developing SSA.*

   If you know a young boy who is surrounded by women and has no healthy masculine role model, either stand in the gap for that young boy, or if you are in a position to talk to his mother, perhaps you might suggest someone to her who can serve as a male mentor for her son. Boys need men to initiate them into the world of masculinity. Mothers cannot do this.

3. *Today, if healthy men would befriend John, love him, and put their arms around him, displaying healthy male affection, eventually his anger and pain would arise. Underneath the rage is a hurting little boy. If you know a SSA man in this situation, embrace his anger, allow him to express his pain, and in so doing, his life will be changed forever. After the rain comes the sun.*

   The natural process of healing is to grieve. Part of that grief may manifest itself in anger, confusion, rage, frustration, fear, or pain. Be there with the man you are mentoring and listen—you don't need to provide answers. Just be there with him as he releases years

of heartaches and pain. Through this process, he will learn to expe-
rience love from healthy men who care without any demand for
sex, without any demand for performance. What a new experience
of love this will be for him, helping to restore his broken heart.

Rosie O'Donnell

I believe that Rosie experiences same-sex attractions, like many other SSA
women, due to a combination of factors:

1 – Hypersensitive temperament

2 – Insufficient mother-daughter bonding / abandonment

3 – Strained father-daughter relationship

4 – Body-image wounds

5 – Sexual abuse

I admire Rosie O'Donnell. I read her autobiography, Finding Me
(Warner Books, New York, 2002), as well as an interview she and her
former partner Kelly did for The Advocate. *Rosie is bright, talented, sen-*
sitive, amusing, vulnerable, caring, articulate, and brave. Her heart of
compassion is matched by her down-to-earth demeanor. Ms. O'Donnell
is a busy woman juggling family life, sponsoring and working with an
adoption agency, championing and speaking out for homosexual rights,
making movies and hosting television and radio shows. After separating
from her former partner Kelly in 2009, Rosie became involved with
another woman.

Ms. O'Donnell's autobiography details many of the causes of her
SSA. By quoting several passages from her book, I will identify why Rosie
is another classic study of why someone might experience SSA.

She was the middle of five children growing up in an Irish Catholic
home in New York. Her mother died of breast cancer in 1973, when

Rosie was just 11 years old. She and her mother have the same name: Roseann. To her friends, she is known as Ro.

Throughout her autobiography, she shares about her involvement with Stacie, who she believed to be a frightened, wounded and pregnant 14-year-old girl who was raped by her pastor. Against the advice of family and friends, Rosie spent many days, nights, and months trying to "save" her. This is a classic co-dependent scenario, trying harder than the other person to get them well. Rosie helps others, but hasn't been able to resolve her own issues. In the end, Rosie found out that Stacie's pregnancy was a "hoax," and in fact Stacie was a deeply traumatized woman named Melissa who experienced dissociative identity disorder (multiple personalities) and created alternate egos to survive a horrific past. Rosie's account of her relationship with Stacie reveals her own fragile state of being.

I have the deepest respect for Ms. O'Donnell for exposing her frailties. It takes a lot of guts and courage to show such vulnerability. With the aim of understanding what might have caused her SSA, I would now like to construct a portrait of Roseann O'Donnell by using her own words. Thanks to her publisher for granting permission to use her many quotes. I will offer suggestions why she developed SSA. I do this in humility and in consideration that Rosie, like all of us, is a wounded soul looking for love and understanding. (Thanks to her publisher for permission to use these quotes.)

HYPERSENSITIVE TEMPERAMENT

Rosie worked with expectant mothers in her New Jersey nonprofit adoption agency. Many reorientation/reparative therapists have observed that those who experience SSA are highly sensitive men and women, responding to circumstances with a heightened sense of emotional awareness and attunement to others' feelings and needs. The shadow or unconscious side of this gift is that most often the individual is not attentive or aware of his or her own needs. Then they seek solace through others, or in the arms of someone else, as their way of saying, "Please take care of me." This is the voice of the child within.

"I know stuff. Stuff I shouldn't. It scares some people. Not me. It started when I was little, before I knew what they were, these ethereal moments where I am given information from some unknown place inside me" (13). "I think I have OCD or ADD or some other three-initial ditty. Whatever it is, it is exhausting" (15). "I can't stand the pain in their voices, the tenderness in their hearts, their struggling souls. Also, I become over involved. To put it bluntly, I have no boundaries. Zero, nada, zippo—none" (5).

INSUFFICIENT MOTHER-DAUGHTER BONDING / ABANDONMENT

Family rule in the O'Donnell house: Don't share your thoughts, feelings or needs (as you may remember, this is the same unspoken code in the alcoholic or high stress family). Rosie was unable to grieve the loss of her Mom. She still has a hole in her soul, longing to experience and obtain her mother's love. This is one contributing factor that may lead to the development of SSA, seeking for maternal bonding with another woman, the "reparative drive." After puberty, this emotional need for bonding becomes eroticized or sexualized. The world then mistakenly says, "You're gay," or "You're lesbian." More accurately, within Rosie is a little girl longing for her mother's love. If you have heard many of Rosie's interviews, she frequently shares about the deep loss of her mother.

"I did not go to my mother's funeral. I went to her wake. It was quite a scene…I saw my stiff sleeping mommy and realized, right then, that she wasn't going to wake up. Then I cried. I cried very hard…On the day I got my driver's license, I went to visit my mother's grave for the first time…I feel I never really got to say a full good-bye. Sometimes I think that may be why I'm still saying good-bye, today. It's like I'm somehow stuck. Mom, Mom. You could just call out forever" (29). "After my mother died, the house and just about everything else fell into total disrepair. It was always dark inside. Life itself was smeared a dull gray. It smelled of dust and stale urine. To me, it smelled of death" (19). "She died. She remains a mystery to me" (23). "There was an awkward silence. Never speak the truth, that's the rule. See her die before your eyes, but say nothing" (26).

STRAINED FATHER-DAUGHTER RELATIONSHIP

In her book, Rosie recalls being estranged from her dad while growing up. He was unable to allow his daughter to express her deeper feelings and support her growth. He was also overwhelmed raising five children alone. Rosie has a negative view of intimacy with men based upon the relationship with her dad and being sexually abused. There is glaringly very little Rosie shares about her relationship with men, only a brief mention of abuse but little else. The omission speaks volumes...most likely, she has much fear of men, but as you see in her appearance, she dresses and acts more masculine herself...identifying with the perpetrator to maintain control and power.

"When I was twenty-nine, I fell in love with a man who was sweet and funny and kinder than any man I had ever known. Tall, blond, and handsome, with a stunning smile, we spoke about getting married, which was both thrilling and repulsive. He didn't care what size my body was and no matter how hard he tried to convince me of that, I never believed him. As he and I got closer, I got bigger. For every pound I gained, I took one step backward, using flesh for padding. I bubble-wrapped my heart...I am difficult to love, and I know it. I never learned the unconditional part, so trust evades me. Add sex and I fall apart, eventually retreating back into the swamp" (73). "I knew nothing of boys, and what I knew of men was no enticement to boy-raising" (157).

BODY-IMAGE WOUNDS

Rosie experiences gender detachment, remaining at odds with her body and femininity. This establishes a pattern to seek self-acceptance by joining with someone of the same gender…in essence, trying to love herself through another woman, trying to obtain a sense of femininity she never adequately internalized while growing up. She is typical of most SSA men and women in that she doesn't like her body. When children fail to sufficiently emotionally attach to the same-gender parent, and/or same-gender peers, they generally reject their own sense of femininity or masculinity. This leads to gender confusion. Rosie, characteristic of many women with SSA, does not like her feminine body.

"Being a girl was horrible and gross. It was the end of the world as I knew it. First I found a lone strand of hair under my arm, and now this [*referring to her menstruation cycle*]. I prayed it was all some sick joke mothers were forced to tell their daughters" (8). "I hate my body. I always have. I hate to admit this fact, but it is just that: a fact. I do not look in mirrors, I try never to be naked. If I could have sex with my clothes on I would. I am the dieting queen, but, along with all the other four billion diet queens in this country, I never stick with the program" (71). "Fat is a protector; anyone can tell you that. I didn't like being 'thin.' I felt like people could come too close" (72).

SEXUAL ABUSE

Many men and women who experience SSA have been sexually abused. I would estimate that half of my SSA clients over the past twenty years were sexually abused. Many scientific studies have been conducted, with their results showing that a high percentage of those with SSA were sexually abused as children. One potential effect of male sexual abuse upon a woman is her fear of intimacy with men, not wanting to be placed in such a vulnerable position again. Turning to someone of the same gender feels safer and comforting. Rosie is also drawn to "save" other female abuse survivors in an unconscious attempt to heal herself (projective identification). However, this never works.

"I was an abused kid. This is something I have chosen not to dwell on in my public life…So, yes, I had been abused, although the details are not important. What is important is that I had, supposedly, dealt with the fallout in therapy. How naïve I was. Abuse is an ongoing saga for everyone who has lived through it (hence my relationship with Stacie). It may start and stop in real time, but in mind-time it goes on forever" (75). "Why was I drawn to Stacie? Oh, a million reasons, one of which was this: a reliving. A sense of shared pain. Talking to her, I felt this pain, my pain, all over again. And although it's hard to admit, I like how it felt. Electric current, real. It made me feel alive, raw, and sad. I am a swamp person, and so was Stacie" (75). "Maybe it's also an abuse thing. When your boundaries have been violated, you just plain and simple stop seeing the space between people, so people's pain becomes your pain and you have to stop it. At the same time, though, codependency is also a distancing ploy; you're so busy trying to save the world out there you forget about the people close to you, and then, last of all, or first of all, you forget about yourself, that you might be the one worth saving" (78).

As Rosie stated, she has a need to "save" others, yet an inability to take care of herself:

"Show me your wounds, and wait for me to come save you. I will…That's me, 'the queen of nice.'…My giving is impulsive, driven by a demon who also happens to have a huge heart. The contradiction exhausts and embarrasses me" (38, 40). "Stacie had many sides, shifts, and splits in her, as I had in me" (51). "As a superhero, I am sworn to serve. I have no choice really. This need to save people is so strange, because it comes from such a warped place inside me: On the one hand, I think I'm powerful enough to really make a difference; it's sheer disgusting narcissism. On the other hand, I feel so powerless, so much like the people I am trying to help, that I blur the line between me and them…And then there was Stacie herself. Stacie, whoever she was, had become a friend and a reflection, a conduit to the pieces of my own past, pieces I was aware of but had not resolved" (123). "I realized that no amount of therapy, giving away of money, or involvement with other wounded travelers would take away my own damage. I knew I had avoided fully experiencing my own past by living in other people's" (129). "The realizations I came to, through this relationship [*with Stacie*], were at once subtle and profound: Saving the world is a lofty goal and an impossible feat. Swimming in others' pain only delays the journey through your own" (208).

Stacie represents Rosie's own wounded, unhealed inner child whom she is unable to embrace directly. Rosie is emotionally stuck, unable to resolve her childhood trauma, thereby reliving it through others. She works to save others (codependent behavior), at her own expense, disconnected from her wounds and needs. Trapped in a life of same-sex relationships and solving other people's problems, Ms. O'Donnell is unable to access and resolve her own core issues. If Rosie would get in touch with her own inner child, work through a program to heal that child within and experience intimacy with women in healthy, non-sexual relationships, she would heal and fulfill her own sense of womanhood and femininity. Then—naturally—same-sex attractions would dissipate as she becomes comfortable in her own skin.

CONCLUSION

In my opinion, Ms. O'Donnell experiences same-sex attractions, like many other women, due to a combination of factors—hypersensitive nature, gender identity confusion, body image wounds, insufficient mother-daughter bonding, distance from father, and sexual abuse. I propose that if Rosie would work through each one of these issues in her life, experience healthy, non-sexual intimacy with women, and heal with healthy men, then she would ultimately resolve her SSA and experience a sense of inner peace, self-worth, and opposite-sex attractions.

Following are suggestions for healing that will help Rosie and women with similar backgrounds:

1. *The direction of Rosie's life would have been changed if, at the time of her mother's death, her father had been better supported by family and friends, and Rosie had been taken care of by a warm, nurturing mother figure.*

   Sexual abuse is devastating to all children. Rosie needed help as a child to deal with all her confused feelings and thoughts after the abuse. As she mentioned, the way of her family was non-communication of their personal feelings and thoughts. After experiencing any form of sexual abuse, make sure your child, family member or friend gets professional help as soon as possible. Those experiences will not disappear with time. As mentioned, time does not heal all wounds; in fact it only buries them deeper.

   Make sure your family is a safe place for children to express themselves, whatever they are going through, whatever they are thinking and feeling. Listen. Be Mr. & Mrs. KYMS = Keep Your Mouth Shut, and just listen. If Rosie had been able to release her sorrow over her mom's loss and be comforted by loving family members and friends, she wouldn't be stuck in a perpetual state of frozen grief today.

2. *Women, SSA women like Rosie need you! They are looking for healthy maternal and sisterly love in the arms of other women. As we've seen again and again, sexual relationships will obstruct the very thing they seek—to be tenderly embraced and to feel safe, satisfying the need of the child within.*

Kevin Jennings

"I became 'Mamma's boy," which is, of course, the worst thing any self-respecting Southern male child can be. I can't remember a time when that wasn't my name. So I guess there was never a time when I felt like I was a normal boy" (*Mama's Boy, Preacher's Son*, Kevin Jennings, Beacon Press, Boston, MA, 2006, p. xii).

Kevin Jennings was the Assistant Deputy Secretary Office of Safe and Drug Free Schools, US Department of Education. In his autobiography, we witness another typical profile of how a hypersensitive boy developed SSA.

As I read Kevin's autobiography, I cried as I learned about his childhood and adolescence. What a sad life he lived without his father, caretaking his mother, taunted and teased by his older brothers, and incessantly mocked by the boys at school and in his neighborhood. Kevin, another very sensitive soul, was stripped of his pride and dignity over and over again. "Trailer trash" is how he felt about himself. A brilliant boy who went on to become a Harvard graduate, and worked for the U.S. Department of Education, Kevin still carries the many wounds from his past which, I believe led him to experience SSA. (I will summarize most of Kevin's life experiences to honor the request of his publisher.)

Here are what I believe to be the causes of Kevin Jenning's SSA:

1 – Emotionally detached from his father, his role model of masculinity

2 – Over-attached to his mother, identifying more with her feminine nature

3 – Constant abuse from his older brothers, further disconnecting Kevin from masculine identification

4 – Continuous mockery by school and neighborhood boys, more reinforcement for male dis-identification

5 – Negative religious messages regarding SSA; constant judgment causing increased shame and guilt for his SSA feelings—feelings that were merely a symbol of his inner turmoil and unmet needs for healthy masculine love

6 – Lack of protection from male teachers and school administrators, which increased his masculine wounding

7 – Hypersensitive temperament, a beautiful characteristic given by God, became a curse because of the unsympathetic environment in which he lived

FATHER WOUND

Kevin's dad was an angry man and his "spankings were painful, always featuring his black belt" (50). *As a pastor, he preached* "hell and damnation." *Kevin feared his dad, who had a very judgmental character. His father preached in the South, and southerners didn't like his* "Yankee accent," *as well as his habit of* "sleeping with the deacon's wives" (6). *He lost many positions because of these facts. According to Kevin, the two things his dad cared most about were God and sports, while Kevin was into reading and studies.*

When Kevin was eight, his father also worked as a construction worker to supplement the family income. They lived in Lewisville, NC. On Kevin's eighth birthday, his dad asked him where he wanted to go and Kevin said the "Y" *to swim. His father, only forty-seven years old, dove into the pool, had a heart attack and died hours later! His mom proceeded to have a nervous breakdown and Kevin was left alone with all his thoughts and feelings. Kevin was led to believe that he was responsible for his father's death. His brothers would tell him so many times.*

At the funeral service three days later, his mother fainted and Kevin began crying. His brother Mike barked, "Don't cry. Be a man. Don't be a faggot" (p. 19). *Kevin stopped crying and learned that being a man meant never showing his emotions, even at his father's funeral.* "Any male who deviated from those standards had a name. That name was *faggot.* That would be me" (p. 19). *He lived in constant fear of reprisal, while name calling and teasing throughout his childhood was the norm. Kevin learned from a young age to repress his grief for his father's death, and to suppress all his feelings. He was consumed with guilt and shame, believing he "killed" his father.*

MOTHER WOUND

Kevin was over-attached to his mother on the one hand, and fearful of her on the other, as she often beat him. From an early age, he also became caretaker of her needs. At three-and-a-half years old, Kevin had whooping cough and went into the hospital in North Carolina. The family was extremely poor, had no insurance, and therefore waited too long to seek medical help. He was placed in an oxygen tent with needles stuck throughout his body. It was an extremely painful time for Kevin. His mother was there throughout the ordeal as a constant source of love and support. However, Kevin stated, "I'm not supposed to be here at all. As Mom would tell me repeatedly throughout my childhood. I was not a wanted child" (p. x). *Kevin felt the pain and burden of not being wanted while seeing his mother struggle to take care of him and his four siblings. I believe this, and many other experiences, led him to feel low self-worth.*

Kevin's Mom was from a poor Appalachian family in Tennessee. She only completed the sixth grade because she was forced to quit school in order to help support her family. Her alcoholic father slapped his wife and kids around, and tried to sexually abuse her and her sisters. Being extremely poor, they often had no place to sleep, and at times would spend nights in abandoned churches. They had no running water or electricity throughout her childhood. His mother picked cotton as a child, did many chores and took care of her siblings. Kevin's mother "hated" her father for these and other reasons. Kevin would hear about this throughout his own childhood. The message was clear: men are mean, men are bad. This message came across to sensitive and impressionable young Kevin as, "Don't be like them, don't be a boy/man, because men are mean and bad and treat women poorly." This kind of accusation emasculates a boy, causing him to put up a defensive wall around his heart towards his own role models of masculinity, his father, brothers, and other boys at school. It also causes him to identify with the feminine, his Mom, and to dis-identify with the masculine, his dad and other men/boys. This created a "double-bind" in Kevin's heart and mind—I can't be a real boy or man because that would further hurt my mom.

After Kevin's Dad died, the family lived on food stamps. His Mother, a proud woman, was humiliated. Kevin had to eat the free lunches provided by the school and felt embarrassed. He was constantly teased by the other kids because of this. "If I said I was hungry, Mom would remind me of how she would wake up crying from hunger as a child, and that her mom would cry too, because often she had no extra food to feed her" (p.35).

Following his father's death, Kevin's Mom pawned her wedding and engagement rings to survive before she got a job working at McDonalds, where she continued to work for most of Kevin's childhood. From the time Kevin was in sixth grade, everyone else had left home, and it was just Kevin and his mother. They lived in a small trailer.

Kevin's Mom gave him a passion for history and learning. He learned about his Confederate ancestors. He would escape his "drab and depressing" life by studying history and sharing with his Mom about their background. Even though they were so poor, she bought him the entire set of Encyclopedia World Books, *which Kevin consumed, reading every volume. Now that his father had passed and his siblings were gone, Kevin became the main focus of his mother's life. He learned to converse with her in an adult-like manner, growing up very fast.*

Kevin devoured books, they were his best friends. From the fourth grade, Kevin was bored by books for his age group and started reading adult books; he preferred non-fiction to novels. His mother was extremely bright, and had been ahead of her classmates in school, but had been forced to quit school after the sixth grade by her dad. She was self-educated, read a lot and watched TV to stay informed, but her lack of schooling was always a source of shame for her. Therefore, she fiercely supported Kevin's thirst for knowledge.

Like Greg, Melissa, John, and Rosie, Kevin used his gifts (intellectual prowess) to obtain attention and affection, but of course this was just more performance-based behavior for Kevin, the caretaker, Kevin the brilliant student, Kevin the little boy who took care of his hurting and lonely mother.

Yet even as hard as he tried to do everything perfectly, Kevin's mother went wild when she spanked him, which would last from a few seconds to ten minutes. She sometimes used belts and very hard kitchen utensils to spank him. Kevin feared her hitting him more than his father because he never knew how long she would go off on him. This demonstrates Kevin's love-hate relationship with his mother. It also increased his desire to take care of her needs, or identify with the perpetrator, because if she was happy, he wouldn't get hit.

SIBLING WOUNDS

Kevin had one older sister and three older brothers. Carol, the oldest, was seventeen years older than Kevin. She received little attention from her father because she wasn't into sports or religion. She rebelled to garner attention. Alan, the eldest, was the kindest to Kevin, but he left when Kevin was quite young. Mike and Paul terrorized Kevin through most of his childhood. He feared their anger and being hit. Kevin lived in constant fear. Name calling and teasing was also the norm.

Again, because Kevin asked his father to go to the Y on his eighth birthday, his brothers thought he was to blame for his father's death. "This wasn't a conclusion I came to on my own. No, my older brothers told me explicitly that it was my fault that Dad was dead" (p. 41). *Kevin's mom was easily upset and his brothers suggested that he might kill her too!* "If I upset my mom—easy to do, as Dad's death and my childhood illness made her more and more jumpy, and an inexplicable absence of more than two minutes would often throw her into a paroxysm of hysteria—my brothers pulled me aside and whispered, 'What are you trying to do, kill your mother like you killed your father?'" (p. 42).

Kevin's brothers used him as a whipping boy, taking out their hurt and pain on him. They also used guilt: besides blaming him for his father's death, they also shamed him into believing that he might kill his mother as well. No child should have to live with such false beliefs. This demoralized Kevin from a very young age. No one was there to defend him. Today, Kevin is the defender of young children throughout the USA.

HYPERSENSITIVE TEMPERAMENT

Kevin experienced a tormented childhood and a hypersensitive temperament that made his life experiences all the more punishing. He did not have the internal strength to fight back therefore he internalized all the negative messages his family and peers threw at him. He always felt shameful about: (1) his same-sex attraction, (2) thinking he was not wanted, (3) believing that he killed his father, (4) imagining that he might kill his mother, (5) being non-athletic, and (6) being a "geek" because he loved learning.

His father tried and failed to get him on a football team with his brothers when he was underage (Kevin was just six, and the starting age was eight). Still Kevin blamed himself since his father couldn't be wrong. He experienced further rejection and self-condemnation. Kevin's sensitive nature was neither honored nor understood by his family members, relatives, or peers. If you read Kevin's autobiography, you can easily observe the similarities between his sensitive temperament and that of Greg, Melissa, John, and Rosie.

MALE PEER WOUNDING

Name calling—"faggot," "queer," "sissy," "teacher's pet," "nerd"—was almost a daily occurrence throughout Kevin's childhood and adolescence. Being non-athletic and the last one picked for teams in gym class, also contributed to feeling left out. Kevin was terrorized on the bus trips to and from school, traumatized by boys after getting off the bus, and teased and mocked during gym class. Meanwhile, by the age of eight, Kevin had lived in seven or more homes! Being the new kid at school is very difficult for any child and was more so for Kevin, being so sensitive. He was also singled out because he lived in trailer parks, and the other kids ridiculed him for this as well.

"Mom and Dad's spankings, and my brother's bullying, would leave their scars in the form of a clear lesson: when people get angry, they hit you. I developed a lifelong, nearly paralyzing fear of angry people, so much so that I would do anything to avoid getting others angry—anything, no matter how damaging it was to me" (pgs. 52-53). *In the sixth grade, after getting off the school bus, a trailer park neighbor made him sit on the curb until he and the other kids were out of sight. Kevin took it, just sat there, not wanting to upset anyone. The kids called him "faggot" and other demeaning words. This was just one of many experiences Kevin endured throughout his early life.*

Kevin developed an immense fear of going to school everyday, which became more and more overwhelming for him during childhood. Kevin gained weight in middle school to avoid dealing with his fears and the incessant daily mocking. One of his brothers called him "Baloney Boy." In gym class, they played "smear the queer" when Kevin got the football, so he experienced verbal and physical "smearing" regularly. He was mocked in the locker room for being overweight. Sound familiar? It's the same story of Greg and John. All of this must have led to body-image wounds, which are typical of so many SSA boys and men.

MALE TEACHER WOUNDING

Nearly all male authority figures had a negative impact on Kevin. Abandoned by his disapproving father, mocked by his older brothers and school classmates, he also felt rejected by his teachers. It wasn't safe for Kevin to become a man. He learned this from his mother, and he experienced it with his dad, brothers, classmates and male teachers.

Not only did the boys tease Kevin in gym class, he was also taunted by Mr. Cultrou, his middle school gym teacher. When Cultrou saw Kevin looking at another boy in gym class, he screamed out in front of everyone, "Stop looking at his legs" (p. 58). *Kevin froze while the entire class stared at him. From that time on, the other kids took Mr. Cultrou's taunting as license to increase their harassment of Kevin.*

Kevin went to the school guidance counselor for help but the man did nothing—simply nothing. No one stood up for Kevin. This pained young boy would later found GLSEN (Gay Lesbian Straight Education Network, as referred to in Chapter One) and become the Safe School Czar for the U.S. Dept. of Education. No wonder Kevin has gone to all this effort to keep other SSA kids safe. But his efforts are terribly misguided because Kevin does not understand the truth about SSA.

RELIGIOUS WOUNDS

Kevin's father preached "hell and damnation" in the "Southern Baptist Church tradition." His son was led to believe that homosexuality was the worst "sin," and experienced constant guilt and shame because of his SSA. In his mind, he was wicked and evil because he could not control his homosexual thoughts. His "God" was punishing and mean, like his pastor-father. There was no hope for him or his salvation, even though he accepted Christ. Kevin lived in constant shame and terror of a punitive God, as he lived in fear of his father, brothers, and boys at school and in the neighborhood.

Kevin's father preached in churches, revivals, and crusades. The family's lives revolved around the church, listening to the elder Jennings' "angry sermons." At six years old, Kevin told his father that he accepted Jesus, but his dad responded by saying that Kevin was too young yet to give his life to Christ. Kevin felt unacceptable yet again, assuming that he couldn't even be "saved" by Christ. Something was fundamentally wrong with him. He believed that he was going to hell.

"My dad and our Father (in heaven) had merged together. Right after Dad's funeral, Mom told me that when people die, they go to heaven, where they look down upon you and know your every thought and every action" (p. 40). *Kevin believed that his father was watching as he masturbated, and knew every thought in his mind. This filled him with a great sense of "shame" and "horror."* "My internal policeman would remind me every day: You are bad. You are bad. You are bad. You are bad. So bad you killed your father and want to kill your mother" (p. 42).

Kevin eventually rejected God altogether, because he had prayed for years for his SSA desires to be removed and they only intensified. He had experienced too much shame and guilt throughout his childhood. Now, he had to rid himself of this uncaring, judgmental god. The guilt and shame were too much for such a sensitive, young boy to contain, so he rejected God and his faith.

It is also important to realize how detrimental the concept of "pray away the gay" truly is. Of course God can remove those desires, but he doesn't, because they are connected to a broken heart in need of healing and healthy love. I also prayed for 25 years for God to remove my SSA.

Finally, I amended my prayer and asked God to reveal the meaning behind my SSA. Then, one by one, the causes became clear, and healing ensued. God always listens. We just need to ask the right questions.

CONCLUSION

After graduating from Harvard and becoming a high school history teacher, Kevin learned about a junior high school student, Robbie, who shot himself in the head after experiencing years of taunting and teasing because of his SSA. "I found myself wanting to find every Robbie in the country and tell him it would be okay, to hang on, that school was the worst part and it would be alright when you got out and could make your own path in life. I started thinking that I needed to view every lesbian, gay, bisexual, and transgender child as if they were my children and fight for them as ferociously as parents like Leslie [Robbie's mother] had fought for theirs" (224). *Kevin has become the voice for the voiceless; however, he has not healed his own wounds as he fights for others (similar to Rosie's journey).*

Kevin was born on May 8, 1963. If you see a photo of Kevin today, or catch him on TV, you would think that you are looking at a much older man. His appearance is saddening. From "trailer trash," to Harvard student, to history teacher, to founder of GLSEN, to US Department of Education, this brilliant and sensitive man is hurting, and hurting others by propagating false claims about homosexuality. Kevin's heart is in the right place, but he lacks a true understanding of what drives his and others' SSA.

Here are suggestions that could help Kevin, and men like him, find healing:

1. *I wish a trustworthy man could hold Kevin in his arms and tell him, "You are wonderful just as you are. You aren't responsible for your father's death. You were not responsible to take care of*

your mom (as a child). Your brother's cruel words only reflected their own pain, projected onto you. The kids in the neighborhood and at school were repeating what they had experienced from their own parents. It wasn't about you Kevin, it was all about them." "You are wonderful. You are strong. You are masculine. It's good to be a boy. It's good to have feelings. It's good to express your feelings and share your thoughts with others." "When anyone speaks about you in a negative way, just look into their eyes, see their own pain, and know that is has nothing to do with you." "You, Kevin, are God's precious son, made in His image. You have so many wonderful unique talents and gifts. You will bring much healing and light into the world." "Kevin, you are loved just for who you are. You don't need to do anything to deserve or earn love. You are loved just for who you are."

As a former SSA boy and man, I understand Kevin from the inside out. As an adult, heterosexual man with three children, two of them young men, I want to express love to Kevin, show him how fantastic he is, and assure him that his SSA is merely a representation and accumulation of so many of the unresolved wounds from his past and legitimate needs for healthy masculine love. "Kevin, sex will never bring you what you truly need," I'd like to tell him. "You need to taste the love of healthy heterosexual men, men who can bless you, men who will have your back, men who will listen to your pain and let you grieve in their arms."

FINAL CONCLUSION

I hope the stories you've read in this chapter will inspire you to reach out to the Kevins, Rosies, Johns, Melissas and Gregs of this world. They are hungrily looking for love. If they'd had healthy male or female mentors while growing up, the outcome would have been entirely different. If we could only begin to set love in order, eventually there would be no children who experience SSA and other wounds of the heart. There are always predictable causes for SSA—and those causes can be avoided or, if necessary, reversed.

I cried many tears reading these celebrities' autobiographies and writing their evaluations. I see them as my brothers and sisters, and I love each one of them. There is no reason why men and women who experience SSA must suffer like they have. We have answers and solutions. We need to spread the truth in love to save lives. The next two chapters will describe how we can rightly love those who experience SSA. But first, Debora's story.

Debora's Story

I am including this particular story because it is representative of those who receive help from religious-mediated ministries and/or church supported change efforts. Since the early 1970s, the mental health profession abdicated responsibility for the scientific investigation about the causes of SSA and successful treatment plans of change for those who experience unwanted homosexual feelings. As a result, many para-church ministries have sprung up around the USA and throughout the world (see a list of international organizations at the back of the book). They have filled a vacuum that the mental health profession created over four decades ago.

Radical transformation is possible! I lived 18 years of my life as a lesbian with absolutely no desire to change. Now that I have been set free, I am experiencing the most wholesome and unconditional love of God, and will never turn back!

I was born in 1963, to a 19-year-old mother and a 21-year-old father who had lost their first child, my older brother, to complications during childbirth less than a year earlier. My parents both came from homes where their same-gender parent died when they were very young. I am the oldest of three biological children of my parents and one adopted sibling. I was brought up in the Catholic Church, and early in my life, I developed a love for God and even dreamed of becoming a nun.

I was extremely insecure as a little girl and did not make friends easily. I never really connected with kids my own age, and my best friends were always older than me. I matured quickly, and beginning at the age of 9, I took on the role of babysitter for my younger siblings as well as the 50 foster children (infants) that my family took in over a period of 7 years. I felt like an adult, even as a child.

In junior high school I began dating a boy who was a couple of years older than I. He lived quite a distance away, so he would come and spend the weekends at my house whenever possible. During this time, my mother started to go with us to the movies or bowling alley nearly every time we went out. She never really dated as a teen because she was raising her two younger brothers. She married my father at the age of 16 to get away from her alcoholic father and her dysfunctional family situation.

When I was 15, my boyfriend and I were away at a church camp and there he tried to have sex with me. When I returned home, I discussed this with a very close family member, through whom I experienced a deep betrayed shortly thereafter. This sent me spiraling.

I built an impenetrable stone wall around my heart and started dressing like a man, making my appearance completely undesirable to men. I befriended my college roommate, and she showed me non-sexual love. We started sleeping together, and she would just hold me, and I felt safe. But I then became extremely jealous when she started dating a man and he moved into our house. I had to endure the pain of hearing them together in the next room, and I was alone once again. I began to struggle with the thought that I was truly a homosexual. I even sought out counseling, and the therapist said that I was a homosexual and should just embrace it.

I entered the Army at the age of 24, and there met a woman who introduced me to homosexuality. At first I felt safe and loved. However, she was involved with another woman as well, and my relationship with her was an emotional rollercoaster ride. During that time, I was also seduced by two different married men who wanted to have sex with me, and I gave in to them because I was looking for love and struggling with who I was sexually. I ended up completely embracing homosexuality and began to live as a closeted homosexual in the military. My first homosexual lover eventually left me after a rocky 6-year relationship, and I spiraled back into deep depression. I truly felt like I would die.

In 1993 I began dating a woman who went to church, and one day she invited me to join her. I said that there was no God and that I hadn't crossed the threshold of a church since I was 15. She looked me straight in the eyes and said, "Jesus wants you back." At that moment, the Lord began to break down the barriers in my heart and I began traveling the road back to him. I personally experienced what the Bible says in Ezekiel 36:26-27: "I will give you a new heart and put a new spirit within you; I will take the heart of stone out of your flesh and give you a heart of flesh. I will put My Spirit within you and cause you to walk in My statutes, and you will keep My judgments and do them."

I joined the Metropolitan Community Church (MCC), a homosexual church. I became indoctrinated in their beliefs that God made me homosexual and that he was pleased with my lifestyle, and I became very involved in the church. Over time, I discovered that the woman who brought me back to church was an alcoholic, and I suffered both sexual and emotional abuse in that six-year relationship. In January 2000, I left her behind and moved to the Washington, D.C., area and sought out another MCC church. I entered into another homosexual relationship in April 2000, and the two of us were warmly accepted by the gay community where we lived. In 2001 we traveled to Vermont and entered into a civil union. We began to build our life together. We bought property and built our dream home, co-mingling everything we owned.

I became unsatisfied with the MCC churches I had found, so I began to seek out other types of churches. My partner and I found a church that we loved the first time we attended service. I was shocked and disappointed to see the word "Baptist" on the sign out front as we left the church that first day. I just knew that "they" would not accept us there. However, we continued to go to that church and were warmly greeted by everyone. We were determined that over time we would bring change to the church and eventually they would openly accept gays as we showed them that our love for each other was pure.

When the church began a church wide Bible study, we opened our home to host a small group study (which was facilitated by a leader in the church), and at the end of that study the church was having a celebration service and invited anyone who wanted to be baptized to sign up. We requested baptism, and were both called into the assistant pastor's office, where he told us he didn't know if he could baptize us since we were living in sin (we had been "ratted out" by the church leader who facilitated the small group in our home). After a long discussion where we both told him that we would walk away from our lifestyle if that is what God told us to do, he agreed to baptize us. That was Nov. 23, 2003.

Over the next 2 years, I became more and more involved in the church. I volunteered as one of the production managers for Sunday morning services, and became heavily involved in the women's ministry. I also developed a love for the Word of God, which is where the REAL transformation in my life began to occur. My partner and I started to read the Bible together every day, and when we would come across passages about homosexuality, she would question me and I would immediately respond with the "real truth" I had learned at MCC about what the scriptures meant. I firmly believed what I had been taught. All the time, unknown to us, the women's ministry leaders at the church were just loving us where we were and praying fervently for our deliverance.

In the fall of 2005, I approached the women's ministry leader and said that my partner and I wanted to "come clean" with the women in our ministry (believing that nobody in the group knew we were gay). She suggested that we meet with the pastor to discuss this before talking to the women's group, so we began a series of meetings with him. The pastor asked me why I labeled myself as homosexual. I answered that I was born that way and felt I needed to tell him who I was because my lifestyle didn't conform to what the church teaches. He said he just saw me as a child of God. They confronted our beliefs in a gentle and loving way, never backing down from their convictions, but gently showing us what the scriptures said about the way we were living. Over time, the Lord convicted us through his word—the Truth.

We decided to follow the Lord at all costs. We were determined to live out what the Bible says in Luke 9:23: "Then He (Jesus) said to them all, if anyone desires to come after Me, let him deny himself, and take up his cross daily, and follow Me." On Jan. 1, 2006, we publicly confessed to the women's group at church that we were turning away from our homosexual lifestyle and following Jesus. We began by moving into separate bedrooms in our house, and eventually, my partner moved out completely. This was an extremely painful time, but we were determined to do what was right. It felt like a physical death, with the loss of physical touch and the struggle to redefine myself. I didn't know who I was anymore, because I had identified myself as a lesbian for 18 years, and at that time had actually convinced myself that I had always been homosexual. I thank God for the healthy heterosexual women who surrounded me with love as I suffered through this transition.

As I drew closer to Christ, he began to reveal to me the things that had occurred in my past that led me to embrace that lifestyle, and God began to heal those deep wounds in me. I also grieved the loss of what my life could have been if I had married and had children, realizing now that I may never marry and have a family of my own.

I cannot begin to tell you how much God has blessed me since I have completely turned away from denying his existence and living a life of homosexuality for a total of 24 years! God did such an incredible thing in me—I feel as if he actually transformed my DNA! Please be encouraged by my story, whether you are struggling with same-sex attraction, or you are a family member or friend of someone who is, because change is possible!

Conclusion

Have you identified some of the causes of Debora's SSA? Here are at least some of them:

1. Debora was detached from and wounded by her mother, her gender role-model of femininity. Debora's mother was an adult child of an alcoholic (ACOA). As we've seen, in the alcoholic family system, experiencing one's feelings, thoughts and desires is not an option. Having missed her youth, she leaned on Debora to help raise her siblings and foster children. Debora also experienced a deep betrayal by a close family member during her teens, which led her to reject God. (Children often reject their parents' belief in God when they reject their parents.)

2. Hypersensitive temperament: Debora was highly attuned to her mother's feelings and that of others. She was a natural caretaker, but this gift was used to win the love and affection of others. Debora became more and more detached from her deeper self.

3. She experienced low-self worth and had no close friends among her own peers. Debora only related to older kids, typical behavior of what is commonly called the "parentified" child. The parentified child knows too much, too soon, and thereby takes on the characteristics and behaviors of an adult.

4. Debora was sexually abused and used by men. She began to dress like a man so as not to be perceived as sexually desirable or attractive to men. The unconscious thinking goes something like this: "Women are weak so I'll act like a man." Of course these thoughts may be completely unconscious. This may have contributed to her gender dis-identification as a woman.

5. Socialization into the homosexual myth. Debora was groomed into lesbianism by women who showered her with attention and affection. She sought her mother's love in the arms of these women.

Suggestions

Here are some ways family members and friends may help a woman like Debora:

1. It is apparent that Debora lacked a healthy relationship with both her mother and father. She never mentioned the participation of her dad in her life. Not only was there wounding with her mother, but her father also left a hole in her heart, not providing her with a healthy image of men.

    In Debora's healing, wonderful women in her church provided the first source of healthy feminine love. This is a beautiful example of how straight women can naturally help SSA women heal and fulfill their innate heterosexual potential.

2. Debora was sexually used by men, seeking to heal the father wound, and finally turned to women for safety and love. She still needs healthy men to demonstrate positive masculine love and concern. As the parentified child, Debora is comfortable taking care of others. It is more threatening to allow others to care for her.

Just as wonderful women began to love and mentor Debora, so men also need to shower her with healthy male affection, restoring the misuse and abuse of her past. Naturally, she may be defensive at first by any attempt of men to display healthy concern and affection. However, in time, with persistent effort, the walls will come down and the love will come in, just as it did with her healthy female mentors.

3. Speak loving words into the lives of those who have either experienced or experience SSA: "I love and accept you just as you are." "You are beautiful and feminine." "I love you Debora." Because she was hurt by her mom, missing a masculine father, and sexually abused by men, she needs lots of positive affirmation from both men and women.

CHAPTER FOUR

Words that Hurt / Words that Heal

We've learned about the potential causes of SSA. We've considered the many wounds and unmet love needs that created those desires. How punishing to someone who is already in pain to hear words like "faggot," "queer," "sissy," "dyke," "pansy," "homo." It's like we are kicking someone who is already down on the ground bleeding, stomping on his or her open wounds!

Can you imagine how terrible they must feel? Remember, no one chose to have SSA; they are the result of many contributing factors. First they experience guilt and shame, struggling to reconcile those desires. During this time school kids, family members, and perhaps those in places of worship call him or her names. What to do? How to survive?

In this chapter, I will present terminology coined by homosexual activists. Many of these words or terms were created through years of research, spending hundreds of thousands of dollars to construct language to help us accept and love people who experience SSA. It bears repeating that SSA is an emotionally based condition. We need to promote love in the *truth*, accepting the SSA person and at the same time helping them reclaim their true heterosexual identity and potential.

Let's look at the strategy behind the activists' terminology and try to introduce new and more helpful language. You will discover how "tolerance, diversity, and equality" must be extended to *both sides* of this issue, to (1) members of the LGBT community, and (2) those who experience unwanted SSA, all coexisting together in mutual respect. To further this goal, I will present LGBT terminology and offer suggestions to increase healing and reconciliation:

- No more hate speech, only loving words
- No more "gay," only SSA
- No more sexual orientation, only heterosexuality
- No more same-sex marriage, only marriage
- No more homophobia or anti-gay, only words and actions that heal
- No more hate crimes, only loving deeds
- No more "LGBT" or "questioning youth," only those who experience SSA
- No more "Love the sinner and hate the sin," only standing with our SSA family members, friends, colleagues, co-workers, and neighbors
- No more "once gay always gay," only "no one is born with SSA" and "change *is* possible."

Words can hurt. Words can heal. We often, unknowingly, wound each other daily with ill-chosen words. Generally we don't think about the meaning of what we are saying or their effect upon the listener. Let us look at the language and terminology commonly used regarding homosexuality, again, language that was carefully crafted by leaders of the LGBT movement to promote acceptance.

Most of their terminology (e.g., gay, lesbian, bisexual, transgender, homophobia, anti-gay, same-sex marriage, sexual orientation, domestic partners, internalized homophobia) is intended to both normalize homosexual behavior as well as create sympathy in our hearts towards those who live a homosexual life. All persons who experience SSA have incurred social prejudice—every one of them. They had to survive and feel some semblance of self-respect. Part of this process took place through the creation of language intended to elevate them to equal status with everyone else. The desired outcome was to experience a sense of dignity amidst bigotry.

For centuries, those who experienced SSA were called derogatory terms. In places of worship, homosexuality was spoken about as the "worst sin" and an "abomination," most often without providing hope or any realistic solution. Having never chosen to have homosexual feelings, they felt trapped and condemned, through no fault of their own.

> LGBT strategists coined new language to normalize homosexuality. They strategically took the emphasis off of homosexual *behavior*—anal sex, oral sex, mutual masturbation, fisting—and placed it solely on homosexual *identity*: "We are born gay; God made us this way; gay is not what we do, it's who we are." Think about the strategy put forth in *After the Ball* by Kirk and Madsen (1989): *Whoever frames the debate wins the debate.*

No more hate speech, only loving words

Words can hurt. Words can heal. In terms of homosexuality, some words that hurt the human spirit are "faggot," "dyke," "sissy," "homo," "pansy," "femme," and so on. If you have spoken any of these or other derogatory terms toward anyone you might have suspected as experiencing SSA, then I recommend you do the following things:

1 – Cease and desist

2 – Apologize and ask forgiveness

3 – Use healing words from now

We either build each other up, or tear each other down. We reap what we sow. Every SSA person has experienced more than enough guilt and shame. It is time we embraced all SSA people in word and deed, whether they choose to live an open homosexual life or seek to resolve their unwanted SSA. All are deserving of our love and respect.

Healing words:

"I love you just the way you are."

"I support and stand with you."

"I think you are wonderful."

"You're a fantastic man."

"You're a beautiful woman."

"Please help me to understand your same-sex attractions."

"Please forgive me for hurtful words I said in the past. How did it make you feel when I said such things?"

No more "gay," only SSA

I suggest that we stop using the "gay" word when referring to anyone who experiences or acts upon their same-sex attractions. The real definition of "gay" is happy. The term was usurped by homosexual activists to describe a person who experiences SSA—but believe me, many with SSA are *not* happy. The "gay" word also denotes that someone has accepted a homosexual identity; therefore, "gay" has become a socio-political statement. When we say, "You're gay," instead of, "You experience SSA," it locks someone into a false identity. No one is essentially born with SSA. There is no such thing as a homosexual (a noun). There are only people who experience same-sex attraction (an adjective describing one's thoughts, feelings, and/or desires). It is important that we separate the person from his or her desires and/ or behavior. We may do this by no longer using the "gay" word, but instead describing him or her as someone who experiences SSA.

Every SSA man and woman is a latent heterosexual stuck in early stages of psychosexual development. When they heal those wounds, and fulfill unmet love needs in healthy relationships, they will experience the fullness of their own gender identity and opposite sex attractions will ensue.

By calling someone "gay," "lesbian," "bisexual," or "transgender," we are reinforcing their woundedness. We do so by keeping them locked up in a false identity, and thereby prohibiting them from maturation and growth into their true manhood or true womanhood. Instead, let's say that he or she experiences same-sex attraction. Begin removing the word "gay" from your vocabulary. Let us call forth all persons who experience SSA into their true heterosexual potential.

Healing words:

"I understand that you experience same-sex attraction."

"I understand that you have homosexual feelings."

"Oh, so you have same-sex attractions, or SSA?"

"I respect and accept you just as you are."

(I will explain in a moment why this last phrase is most important.)

I am fully aware that most "gay" identified men and women are not aware of the term "SSA." Most people under the age of thirty have been co-opted into the "born gay and cannot change" myth. The purpose of introducing new language is twofold: (1) to reframe the homosexual issue—no one is essentially born this way and change is possible, and (2) to bring the homosexual issue back into the realm of psychology and spirituality.

No more sexual orientation, only heterosexuality

The term "sexual orientation" was created by members of the Gay Rights Movement to gain public acceptance, while subtly indoctrinating us into believing that people are born with SSA. If it's a "sexual orientation," the implicit meaning is that someone has been this way from birth. You may remember the term "sexual preference" which was introduced into our culture previous to the coining of the phrase "sexual orientation." Homosexual activists realized that using the word "preference" implied choice. Therefore, they quickly discarded that term and replaced it with "sexual orientation," which implies that one's sexuality is not chosen but fixed and cannot be changed. I suggest that we stop using the false paradigm "sexual orientation." It is grossly inaccurate and misleading, having no real basis in science or religion.

By the way, don't let LGBT activists try to convince you that homosexual behavior is natural in the animal kingdom. This is a gross distortion of situational behavior that takes place within certain species. "Preferential homosexuality is not found naturally in any infrahuman mammalian species. Masculine/feminine differences and heterosexual preferences are quite consistent up through the phylogenetic scale" (W. Gadpaille, "Cross-Species and Cross-Cultural Contributions to Understanding Homosexual Activity," *Archives of*

General Psychiatry 37, 1980, pgs. 349-356). "Although homosexual behavior can indeed be found in the animal kingdom, it is not the rule, and when observed, is unusual" (Phelan, J. E. (1998), "Deviated copulation among animals," *Journal of Evolutionary Psychology, 19*(1-2), 41-50).

Healing words:

"We are all heterosexually designed. Men and women fit perfectly together."

"I understand that you are attracted to people of the same sex, but nonetheless I believe that you are inherently heterosexually designed."

"Changing from same-sex attractions to opposite-sex attractions is possible!"

No more same-sex marriage, only marriage

The term "same-sex marriage" sounds like a fluffy new flavor ready to grace your palette. It is meant to normalize homosexual behavior—anal sex between two men, oral sex between two men or two women, mutual masturbation between those of the same gender. As we have already learned, people who engage in homosexual activity are like little kids in adolescent or adult bodies, looking for lost or unattained love. It is a cruel and unreasonable action for us to endorse something that will ultimately betray the very essence of these men and women, prohibiting them from achieving the fullness of their innate heterosexual potential.

One who follows the path of least resistance says, "OK, let them do what they want to do in the privacy of their own homes. It has nothing to do with me." But alas, it may have everything to do with you and your family. What if you unknowingly marry such a person, have a SSA child, relative, or close friend? Then, it hits home! How about future generations? Do you want your children and grandchildren being solicited into homosexual behavior?

We need to stand with and for people who experience SSA, and love them to life. Please do not inadvertently endorse a behavior that would hurt a family member or friend, or enroll future generations into a false way of living. I recommend that we not use the term "same-sex marriage" again. Remember the story of *The Emperor's New Clothes*…speak the truth.

Healing words:

"I am neither homophobic nor anti-gay. I love all people who experience SSA."

"I do not believe that homosexual behavior will help an individual fulfill her or his potential."

"I believe that people are not born with same-sex attraction, and therefore they can change and fulfill their heterosexual potential."

"I believe in natural law, that marriage is meant to be between a man and a woman."

I fully appreciate the fact that presently there are many LGBT couples. However, I am not commenting on this phenomenon as a human rights issue. Our path now is to promote true healing for all who experience SSA and be agents of real love in the world.

No more homophobia or anti-gay, only words and actions that heal

Homophobia: "Irrational fear of, aversion to, or discrimination against homosexuality or homosexuals" (Merriam-Webster's Medical Dictionary, 2002).

Phobia: "An extreme and often unreasonable fear of some object, concept, situation, or person" (American Heritage New Dictionary, 2005).

Homo: "'The same,' prefix commonly used to form modern words, from Greek homos 'one and the same'" (Online Etymology Dictionary, © 2001).

Anti-gay: "Opposed or hostile to homosexuals or to homosexual social reforms and institutions" (Dictionary.com, Based on the Random House Dictionary, 2010).

The term "homophobia" is grossly misused and misunderstood. LGBT activists created this term to make themselves appear as victims by anyone who does not endorse their homosexuality and homosexual behavior. Brilliant, but wrong! We love those who experience SSA while having a principled disagreement with their homosexual behavior; these two concepts are not mutually exclusive. Disagreeing with their behavior does not make us "homophobic," fearful or condemning. One is not "homophobic" because he doesn't approve of a behavior that he thinks would do harm to the individual. In such a case, there is only a difference of opinion, accompanied with love and respect.

We also need to challenge the false concept of "anti-gay." Much like the term "homophobia," one is able to love all SSA persons without endorsing their choice to live a homosexual life. SSA persons have a choice to act upon their desires or to seek change. Their SSA feelings were not optional, but what they do with them is.

> Healing words:
>
> "I may not agree with your homosexual behavior, *but* I love you just as you are!"
>
> "I love all people who experience same-sex attraction."
>
> "Please do not label me with such a term just because I do not agree with you. We are all entitled to our own opinions. I respect yours, please respect mine."

There is also the term "internalized homophobia," which is assigned to someone who has internalized negative social or religious attitudes towards his or her own or someone else's homosexuality. Again, this is a false and confusing term, created to promote a one-sided argument. I may disagree with someone's homosexual behavior and love him or her at the same time. Do not accept the term "internalized homophobia" if you do not approve of a specific behavior. This is reverse discrimination rearing its ugly head!

> Healing words:
>
> "I love you just as you are."
>
> "I may not approve of your behavior, and I still love you!"
>
> "I have a different understanding than you. I respect your opinion, so please respect mine. Let's both practice true tolerance, real diversity, and equality for both sides of this issue!"

No more hate crimes, only loving deeds

We must stop all discrimination against SSA persons, whether they decide to live an open homosexual life or seek change. Words and deeds either kill or uplift the human spirit. *Let us be change agents in the world!* World peace begins with me, my family, and my community. If you see anyone acting violently towards a SSA person, if possible attempt to stop them or contact the police. Defend those who need defending. You could save someone's life. If you hear anyone speaking disparagingly about a SSA person, kindly correct them.

Healing words:

"It hurts me when you speak about same-sex attracted people in such a way. I have learned that they are not born this way. They do not choose to have same-sex attraction, or SSA. They may change from SSA to straight if they decide to. I know of people who came out of homosexuality and are living their heterosexual dreams."

"Excuse me. Please do not use those words around me. I know people with same-sex attraction, and it hurts both them and me when you say such things."

"Would you want people to speak about you in such a way? I am sure you didn't mean to hurt anyone, but those kinds of words do. Thank you for understanding."

No more "LGBT" or "questioning youth," only those who experience SSA

We have discovered already that LGBT terminology was created to gain public acceptance for those who experience SSA. Kirk and Madsen's Homosexual Manifesto (*After the Ball*, 1989) set the wheels in motion to increase acceptance but not a real understanding about homosexuality. *We are straight and late.* Now it is time to catch up and set love in order. It is time to speak words that promote real healing in the world.

We need to turn things around now, much like the desensitization, jamming and converting strategies we've learned about. Let's stop using terms such as "lesbian," "gay," "bisexual," "transgender" or "questioning youth." When we say the word "homosexual," there is a visceral experience in our body letting us know something in incongruent. Sit for a moment, and repeat the word "homosexual" five times. How does it feel? There is almost always cognitive dissonance when we say the word "homosexual."

Now say the word "gay" five times? How does that feel? When you say the word "gay," there is a pleasing, pleasurable physical and emotional sensation in your body. I know that most of us have been anesthetized by the "gay" and "lesbian" terminology (through the process of desensitization). This word was chosen to promote the acceptance of a homosexual identity. Now it is our time to *reframe* the issue. Anyone who experiences SSA is not "gay," "lesbian," "bisexual," or "transgender;" they are all latent heterosexuals.

Are you wondering, what is a "bisexual," or is there really such a thing? The simple answer is, "No." Anyone who experiences attractions for both men and women is stuck in an early stage of psychosexual development. It means that there may have been some degree of bonding with either the same-sex parent and/or same-sex peers, but obviously it was insufficient. The byproduct is attractions to both men and women. He or she may have also experienced some wounding with members of the opposite sex. There are always reasons locked within the human psyche that explains such a phenomena. Once again, one and one equals two, men and women fit together;

two men, or two women simply do not. My personal and professional experiences are that SSA is always a symptom of unresolved issues and unmet love needs. If someone is attracted to both men and women, they hold some wounding in their mind and heart, and when released, heterosexual desires alone will emerge.

You may wonder, "If someone comes out of homosexuality, will they, like others in recovery, have to struggle throughout their lives with those desires?" It's the wrong question because of an incorrect understanding about SSA. Homosexual feelings are the result of specific unresolved wounds from the past, and unmet legitimate love needs (for healthy male or female bonding). If someone experienced childhood sexual abuse, engaged in homosexual behavior before adolescence, and/or viewed homosexual porn from a young age, then neural pathways in their brains were created equating intimacy with sexual activities. Through repeated behavior, these neural patterns became strengthened. In the healing process—when one resolves past wounds, and fulfills basic love needs in healthy, non-sexual same-sex relationships—those attractions diminish and opposite-sex desires emerge. However, if such an individual is under stress, those old neural patterns may reemerge, as a fallback, a way to medicate or block emotional pain. This does not mean they will "struggle" with SSA. It is only past neurological patterns resurfacing, and as I tell all my clients, this is a message from your soul merely attempting to get your attention. Once the individual understands what was troubling him or her, the SSA dissipates, sometimes within seconds.

Another word to avoid is "transgender." Those who believe themselves to have been born the wrong gender harbor profound wounding in their soul. One such gentleman came to our office for help. He looked and acted like a woman, having had hormone injections for several years that increased his breast size. He was contemplating reassignment surgery (removing his penis and building a vagina). He taught me a lot about how such men and women feel. "As a man, no one listened to me or took me serious. As a woman, now I have their attention and people respect what I have to say." He felt mistreated and disrespected as a man (having been called every derogatory name in the book from childhood, both at school and in church). Because of his hypersensitive soul, he didn't have the strength to stand up and push back. Also, he feared his father and gender-identified with his mother and sisters. He wanted to be like them, while craving the attention and affection of men.

His parents actively participated in his healing process. His dad learned how to love this sensitive young man, accept him for who he is, and spend time together. Other men in the community also came around him, pouring healthy masculine love into his hungry spirit. Many repented for horrible acts of bigotry toward him when he was young. They grieved and healed together. Today, this young man no longer takes hormone injections. He has a beard and once again identifies himself as a man. Change *is* possible!

And here's another term to avoid: "questioning youth," referring to adolescents who might be confused about their sexual identity. Scientific studies show that at least 25% or more of teens question their sexuality because it is a very fragile time of psychosexual development. With the high rate of divorce and kids growing up in single-parent families, it is understandable that many question their sense of identity and sexuality. LGBT activists are trying to solicit fragile and confused teens into believing they might be SSA and therefore adopt a homosexual identity.

No more "questioning youth!" Let's speak instead about confused children who need mentoring and the right kinds of love to help them navigate through their adolescent years successfully. Many adolescents experiment sexually with their friends. This does not mean that they are homosexual or experience SSA. Going into adolescence boys are naturally closer to boys and girls with girls. They often experiment with each other before moving into their full heterosexual identity.

The mantra of the homosexual community is "tolerance, diversity, and equality." For 27 years I have been involved in this field as a sexual orientation therapist. I have spoken on university campuses, scientific symposiums, religious conferences, as well as numerous media interviews. Homosexual activists have attended many of these events or participated in the interviews, screaming at me, speaking with anger and espousing abusive words. One of their tactics is character assassination: criticize the messenger so people will not hear the message.

I am a man of love, compassion, and conviction. I have never spoken ill against "gay" identified persons. I lived that life. I would never utter such hurtful words. What I do is share possibilities of change. I respect the right of self-determination and autonomy for every man, woman, and adolescent—deciding to live a homosexual life, or deciding to explore the possibility of change: Life, liberty, and the pursuit of happiness.

Many who demand "tolerance, diversity, and equality" have themselves become the most intolerant individuals. They are critical and condescending toward anyone who does not agree with their viewpoint. Every time I give a presentation or engage in an interview, and face those who mock me or condemn my work, I turn off the volume, look into their eyes, and see a wounded child crying out for love. There he is, hurting and angry, "Please love and accept me." There she is, "Help me, I am in such pain." There is either love or lack of love.

Healing words:

"People who experience SSA."

"No one is essentially born with same-sex attraction."

"I believe in true tolerance, real diversity, and equality for all people."

"Tolerance swings both ways! Equality and justice for all!"

"Each man and woman who experiences SSA has a civil and human right to decide if they wish to live a homosexual life or seek change and come out straight."

"Are you against an individual's human right?"

"Are you against their right of self-determination?"

There's another phrase I hope you will avoid. I highly suggest *never* speaking to a "gay" identified person with the words "I love you, but not your homosexuality;" or "I love you but not your homosexual behavior." This all boils down to "Love the sinner but hate the sin." This does not work with this population because they have been indoctrinated into believing, "God made me gay." "God made me a lesbian." "I'm born this way and cannot change." This has been the systematic mental programming over the past four decades. To them, homosexuality is not just what they *do*, it is who they *are*, the very essence of their being. Therefore, in this instance, the concept of separating the sin from the sinner *does not work*. We have to understand their viewpoint and love them intelligently.

With this understanding, I suggest saying the following words exactly as written, "I love you just the way you are." These eight magic words communicate your unconditional love without any conditions or stipulations. Your family members or friends do *not* need to change in order for you to accept and love them. Don't worry if they misinterpret what you say, assuming that you are endorsing their homosexual behavior. Let them think what they want. If they ask, "Does that mean you accept my homosexual behavior or homosexuality?" Smile and say, "No, and I love and accept *you* just the way you are." Be sure you smile when you say that. This will create cognitive dissonance in their mind because you are now demonstrating unconditional love while disagreeing with their actions. *That is higher love. That is real love.*

Healing words:

"I love you just the way you are."

For four decades we have been inundated through the media, movies, television, schools, politics, and in some instances from various faiths, with the homosexual myth—"born gay and cannot change; once gay always gay." It is time to dismantle this man-made social construct. Kirk and Madsen, and other homosexual strategists, did a fine job in their efforts to stop socialized prejudice. This is a wonderful achievement of the LGBT movement. But somewhere along the line they buried the truth from themselves! We need to dismantle the lies and replace them with real facts about SSA.

Healing words:

"I don't believe that you were born with same-sex attraction. I have learned that people can and do come out of homosexuality. Change *is* possible!"

Conclusion

I strongly recommend that we stop using terminology that was created to promote the acceptance of homosexuality and start using language that uplifts, embraces, and restores these fine and sensitive men and women. In this way, we become part of the solution every time we speak. Be an ambassador of true tolerance, real diversity, and equality for all.

No more hate speech, only words of apology and love. No more "gay," only SSA or same-sex attraction. No more "sexual orientation," only heterosexuality. No more "same-sex marriage," only marriage! No more "homophobia," "anti-gay," or "hate crimes," only words and deeds that demonstrate love and acceptance while fully understanding the meaning behind SSA. No more "LGBT" or "questioning youth," only people who experience SSA, and are essentially latent heterosexuals. No more "love the sinner and hate the sin," only, "I love and accept you just as you are." No more "once gay always gay," but instead, "change *is* possible for those who wish to come out straight!"

Let us reframe the debate. Make a clear distinction between homosexual *behavior* and homosexual *identity*. Every time we use the "gay" word, we reinforce a false concept of homosexuality and imprison people. As Gandhi eloquently stated, "Be the change you wish to see in the world." Sam's story is a wonderful example of change, made possible by a loving and godly mentor.

Sam's Story

This is a beautiful story about the power of mentoring. A wonderful man intervened in Sam's life and dramatically altered his destiny. Enjoy reading about the power of love.

I was either insane, trusting, or being driven by God to talk to Sarge. He was a three-tour Army vet, complete with a Purple Heart and other medals. I had completed one tour. We were in Virginia. I was going through school, and he was one of the instructors.

I'd gotten to know Sarge because I was being selected to stay on and attend school and become an Army instructor for parachute rigging. I could sew well, and I was a meticulous packer. I was also attracted to other men but had been keeping away from gay bars and sexual association on the advice of a therapist I had been seeing prior to being drafted into the Army. I had been an active homosexual from the age of 14 until I was drafted at 19.

I was on an airplane back to Seattle from San Francisco. I had been there because on my 17th birthday when I told my mom I was gay, she sent me, as a gift, to live with three gay men she knew in San Francisco. I had a great time there … but on the plane trip back I was seized with the question, "Why am I queer?

I spent time reading Freud, Adler, B.F. Skinner, and others and began to understand some of the issues. This was 1967, so psychologists didn't encourage anyone to experiment and accept the feelings. I met with one therapist who started working with me, but then I was drafted.

The Army was good for me. When asked if I was a homosexual, I said no. And through boot camp and Ranger school, I was following the advice of my therapist. I still had feelings for men from time to time, but the urges seemed under control.

And then there I was, sitting outside a packing shed with this Sergeant, and I started telling him how I felt about men. That I was attracted to them, that I had a dad who ignored me, a stepfather who terrorized me, and an uncle who locked me in a closet, and on and on. Why did I trust him? God knows. But there I was. And when I finished and was getting up to run away, he said,

"Ya know something, Son? Y'all ain't queer. You just need a real daddy."

"Yeah, right," I said.

"No, y'all need someone to show you how to be a man."

"I am a man," I responded.

"Well, ya sort of are. You're part way there. ... Y'all come over for dinner. This ain't no place to talk, all right?"

So I went to dinner at his home. He and his wife said grace. I didn't believe in any god, as my parents were atheists and so I had grown up without a divine influence, albeit a fairly moral one. My father was an objectivist ... Ayn Rand's philosophy.

After dinner he and I sat outside and we started talking. He just pretty much listened without judgment or comment.

"Y'all need to come over here on Saturday and help me."

"Doing what?" I asked.

"I build birdhouses for the church sales, and I need you to cut wood and paint. By the way, ya know there ain't no queer deer, don't ya?"

"What?"

"God didn't make no queer deer. Takes two to make babies."

"OK ..."

"A man needs to know that he's responsible for his family, needs to have a family in order to become more of a man. ... Any of your homosexual friends grownups? You ain't got to answer now. I just want you to think about it. ... See you for dinner on Saturday. Bring your manners with you."

And this started a routine of me coming over for Saturday dinners as well as Friday nights. Sarge used to tell me, "Y'all get them feelings for a man, you come to the house. We'll just talk, and I'll put you to work cutting wood and painting, and we'll have a beer." When I asked why a Southern Baptist had beer in the house, he said, "Well, Son, I don't hide it from the Lord. I don't get drunk. I like a cold beer now and then, and if I know a fellah's got a problem with his likker, then I offer him lemonade."

Sarge taught me how to fish and how to make birdhouses. His wife taught me how to make buttermilk biscuits and how to be a man toward women. I was always invited to church socials and to services on Sunday. Sometimes I went, but I was not convinced.

Sarge helped me get my license for parachute rigging and introduced me to skydiving. He took me hunting with other vets and showed me how to whittle a bit. He never told anyone that I was struggling, but he'd ask me how I was doing with my feelings.

"Y'all are gettin' better these days. I seen you lookin' at the cute forklift driver the other day."

"Her name is Susan," I said.

"You think she's pretty?" asked Sarge.

"Beautiful red hair, green eyes, and shapely, too," I reported.

Sarge replied, "You sure you used to like boys? You startin' to sound like a lusty fellow to me!"

"I seem to be thinking about that from time to time," I said.

"Well you know there's a proper time for all that sex, don't you?"

"Yeah, yeah. Mrs. B told me it waits till marriage."

"God says so, too. And though I know you ain't one to talk much about God, I want you to think about Him. I'd like you to know Him personally, too. I got some books for you, cuz I know you're a thinker. …"

He'd bought some books by Francis Shaeffer and C.S. Lewis for me, and a Bible with lots of ribbons in it marking passages. These were my birthday presents from him and his wife. "You got some reading to do …"

I put the books away.

I spent almost two years going to see Sarge, building birdhouses, talking, fishing, going out into the woods for one reason or another. We played catch, rough-housed, and went shooting. Basically I found a dad I could love. When I left for school, he asked about the books. I promised I'd read them. I did. It would be years later before I became a Christian. But I'd stopped having sexual attractions for other men. I knew Sarge and his wife had prayed many a prayer over me. He used to hug me and kissed me on the cheek on the rare occasion. As far as I know, only he and his wife knew of my struggle. They did what no one had done before: loved me, listened to me, helped me as I struggled, and provided for me a stable home and a steady diet of love. I also learned that a man could do many things like cook, sew, and paint and still be a man of character with leadership qualities.

Sergeant Balderidge died about twenty years ago, and his wife followed shortly thereafter. But he had pictures of me, my wife, and my two children on his piano at home. To him, I was his son.

Conclusion

I know more details about Sam's history than those he has related. Here is what I believe caused him to experience SSA:

1. Sam was deeply traumatized by his father and stepfather. There was emotional, mental, and physical abuse. Therefore, he never bonded with a healthy male role model before meeting Sarge.

2. Sam was over-attached to his mother, and thus he had internalized her femininity. As we have learned through the other stories, many SSA boys are close to their moms and more distant from their dads. This precludes them from experiencing their own male gender identity. Instead they over-identify with women and their femininity.

3. Sam was hypersensitive. This temperament led to his feeling different from the other boys at school. As a result, he felt like an outcast, looking in and wanting to belong. Being in the military was actually very healing for him. There, for the first time in his life, he belonged, and he fit in with other guys.

4. After puberty, Sam's legitimate need for male bonding became erotized. Then he engaged in numerous homosexual relationships. However, this never satiated his deeper need for bonding, connection and acceptance by healthy men.

Suggestions

How family and friends can help a man like Sam:

1. The Sarge demonstrated what I have been sharing throughout the book: Reach out, embrace, listen and love the unloved. Be a father to the fatherless. Be a mother to the motherless.

"Restore the years the locusts have eaten" and SSA strugglers will eventually come into the fullness of their true gender identity.

2. Sam lived a homosexual life. It didn't work. Finally, with the help of Sarge, he experienced his own power as a man. When a guy feels his own "guyness," no longer will he need another man to complete him. Opposites attract. If a man feels his own masculinity, then he will be drawn to the opposite, a woman. This occurred in Sam's life.

3. Sam's SSA subsided when he was surrounded by men. If you want to help someone come out of SSA, surround him or her with positive and healthy gender role models. The homosexual community has created many venues for SSA people to gather and feel accepted. It's time for us to do the same, but this time, by demonstrating real love.

CHAPTER FIVE

Loving Those with SSA the Right Way

Darkness cannot drive out darkness; only light can do that.
Hate cannot drive out hate: only love can do that.

Martin Luther King, Jr.

My friend was drowning. He was sinking fast. I jumped into the lake, put my arm around him, pulled him to the surface, and swam to shore. After performing CPR, he slowly regained consciousness and began to breathe. I saved my friend's life!

So it will be when you put your arm around someone who experiences SSA. You can help save someone's life. Remember the pain Greg Louganis, Melissa Etheridge, John Amaechi, Rosie O'Donnell, and Kevin Jennings experienced while growing up. They were drowning, and no one came to pull them out of the water. Today, they are in a *trance*, indoctrinated into the homosexual myth. We can actively help them—and those like them—heal and fulfill their innate heterosexual potential. *Change is possible!*

This book is a primer, a Homosexuality 101 course, as it contains the basic facts about SSA—how the homosexual movement gained so much ground in such a short period of time, the hidden meaning behind same-sex attraction, why some celebrities experience SSA, new language to promote healing, and finally practical strategies to love those with SSA the right ways and thereby solve the homosexual dilemma.

Many of us were simply ignorant about the facts regarding SSA—no one is essentially born this way, no one simply chooses to have SSA, and change is possible—and perhaps spoke disparaging words about homosexual persons. With greater knowledge come new opportunities to become part of the solution. In this chapter, I will offer simple suggestions and strategies to set love in order and heal the brokenhearted:

- Apologize for wrong doing, thinking, and speaking
- Spread the truth about SSA
- Love those with SSA the right ways

Apologize for wrong doing, thinking, and speaking

Instead of condemning, mocking, or blindly endorsing homosexual behavior, we need to understand their situation and apologize for any wrongs we might have committed out of ignorance. Please take responsibility for any harsh words or hurtful actions:

Healing words:

"I am very sorry for what I said [name specific words]."

"I am sorry for what I did [name specific behavior]."

"Would you please forgive me?" [After apologizing, say the following:]

"How did my words or behavior make you feel?"

After you ask for forgiveness, please be sure to listen to what your SSA friends or loved one has to say to you. You don't need to have all the answers. All you need is to hear them. Listen to their heart, their pain, and their journey. Most of us don't want advice, we just need to be heard and accepted for who we are. That is one of the greatest gifts we can offer to another human being. Listen without judgment and accept them just as they are.

Don't be surprised if your SSA friends don't want to open up. They may not feel safe at first, and that's OK. Just apologize without expectation. Let them know that if and when they are ready to share, you will be there for her or him.

Another key to enhance communication is to ask, "How did my words or behavior make you feel?" This is an invitation for the SSA person to reveal his/her heart more deeply. Just listen, be Mr. or Mrs. KYMS: Keep Your Mouth Shut! Just listen. It bears repeating: no answers are required. Be a good listener to what they have experienced. As the Beatles sang, "All you need is love. All you need is love. All you need is love, love. Love is all you need!" This time, you love in full knowledge about the truth of SSA.

Healing words:

"Thank you for what you've said. Again, I apologize for any pain that I have caused you. If you have anything else to share, I am here for you. I love and accept you just as you are."

Realize that those who have adopted a "gay" identity believe they were born that way; therefore, do not frame your apology around the causes of their SSA because they do not believe such things… yet! Simply apologize for hurtful words or deeds. That's it, that's all.

Dr. Elaine Segal, a psychologist in New York City, wrote a book entitled *Female Homosexuality: Choice Without Volition.* In her book she recounts working with a group of self-proclaimed lesbians who had no intention of coming out of homosexuality. However, due to successful therapy with several of these women, one by one, they began to lose their SSA and develop heterosexual attractions!

If the man or woman you are listening to gets angry, that's a good thing. Underneath all psychological anger is hurt and pain. Eventually, after they start running out of steam, the tears may begin to flow. Be patient, allowing her to release years of heartache. Basically, it has nothing to do with you, it's about her pent up emotions—feelings you never knew about. You are providing a safe place for her to blossom and grow.

Healing is like peeling an onion. There are many layers around the human heart as depicted in the diagram on the next page, "Layers of the Personality."

This chart describes how our childhood wounds manifest in our lives through adaptive behaviors (this relates to all of us, not just those who experience SSA). Since none of us has experienced ideal parenting or perfect sibling and peer relationships, we all have emotional/mental scars. Those scars will manifest in our adolescent and adult behaviors in various ways and in different social settings. This chart describes some of our coping mechanisms, consequential behaviors and symptoms in our lives.

At the core of one's being is his or her God-given authentic self, full of love, understanding, and forgiveness. Many people of faith believe that we too are born with a "fallen nature," a propensity to do wrong. We are also born with an inherited nature from our ancestors—a composite of their victories and failures.

LAYERS OF OUR PERSONALITY

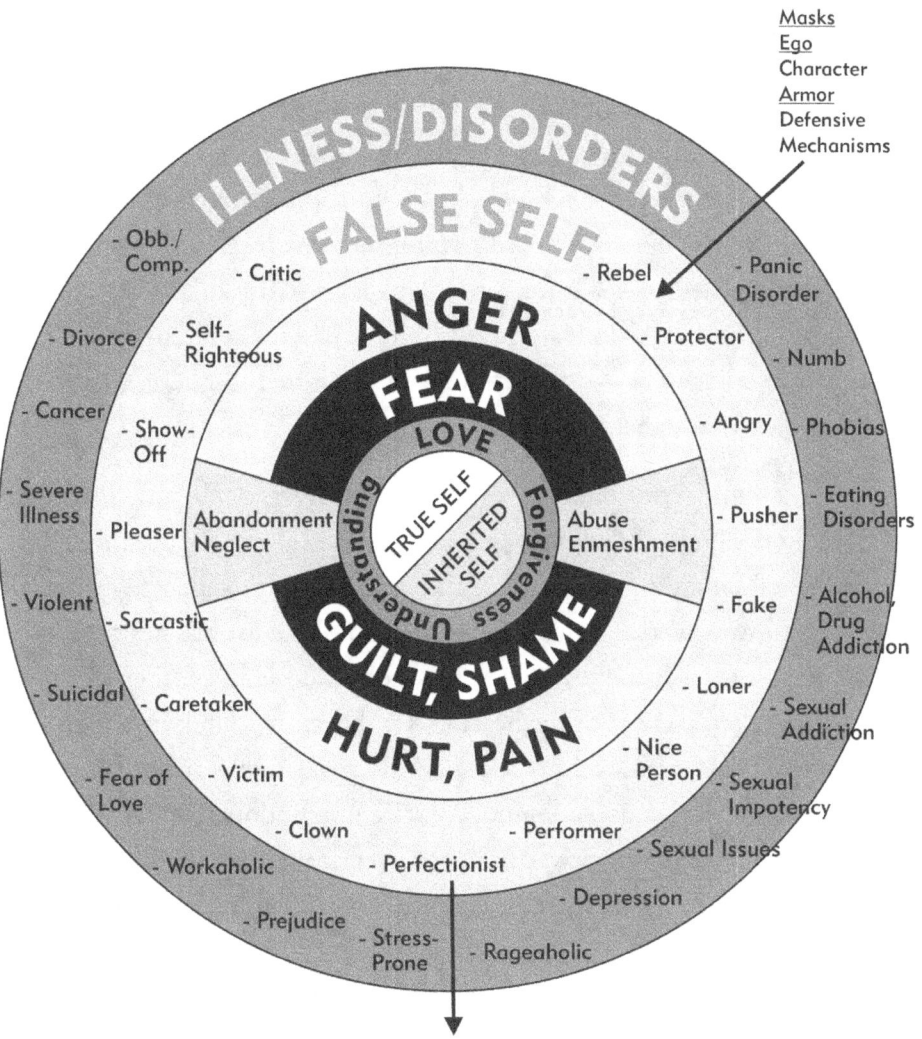

Masks
Ego
Character
Armor
Defensive
Mechanisms

ILLNESS/DISORDERS
FALSE SELF

- Obb./Comp.
- Critic
- Rebel
- Panic Disorder
- Divorce
- Self-Righteous
- Protector
- Numb
- Cancer
- Show-Off
- Angry
- Phobias
- Severe Illness
- Pleaser
- Eating Disorders
- Violent
- Sarcastic
- Pusher
- Fake
- Alcohol Drug Addiction
- Suicidal
- Caretaker
- Loner
- Sexual Addiction
- Fear of Love
- Victim
- Nice Person
- Sexual Impotency
- Workaholic
- Clown
- Performer
- Sexual Issues
- Prejudice
- Perfectionist
- Depression
- Stress-Prone
- Rageaholic

ANGER
FEAR
LOVE
Understanding
Forgiveness
TRUE SELF
INHERITED SELF
Abandonment Neglect
Abuse Enmeshment
GUILT, SHAME
HURT, PAIN

Affection, Affirmation, Acceptance

© Richard Cohen, M.A., January 1999
Counselors Training Program

201

The first layer of wounding you see on this chart is the experience of different forms of emotional hurts: abandonment, neglect, abuse, and/or enmeshment. If a parent gets angry, if there is fighting in the family, if the child perceives being abandoned, any of these and other hurtful experiences will create *fear*. Underneath all psychological fear are two things: guilt and shame. Guilt comes from violating one's set of values and ethics: *I did something wrong; I was bad*. Shame comes from a feeling or thought that I am flawed, that something about me is unacceptable: *I am wrong; I am bad*. That is what a child may perceive while internalizing his or her *fear*. If the child is allowed to grieve and share openly, she or he will heal immediately. If the child is not permitted to share freely, if Mom is too busy or Dad is not around, if Dad and Mom are angry, or if the child is ignored—whatever the case may be—if the child is not permitted to grieve, she or he will internalize her or his *fear*.

If a child continues to experience hurt through any form of abuse, being abandoned, experiencing neglect, or becoming enmeshed (enmeshment, once again, is an over-attachment) with a parent or caregiver, and this child is not allowed to express her or his feelings or express them sufficiently, s/he will develop another layer of defense around her or his heart and mind: *anger*. Underneath all psychological *anger* are hurt and pain. If *anger* is experienced in a healthy way, it is acute, a temporary state of emotional arousal that goes away after the perceived threat is over. If we continue to experience sustained *anger* as a child, adolescent, or adult, it is masking hurt and pain. We were created for love, and for the natural expression of all our emotions. If our parents or caregivers are unable to receive our *anger*, which only masks our hurt and pain, then we become more ill at ease within ourselves. Feelings buried alive never die; they grow and fester under the surface, causing us to develop maladaptive behaviors for survival.

The next layer is what we call the *false self* and consists of the masks that we wear to survive in the world around us. The interesting thing about the false self is this: Our masks or defensive mechanisms often reflect our God-given talents and gifts. However, we then use those abilities to get the love that we needed: affection, affirmation, and acceptance. If I am academically inclined, I may study hard and excel to receive love and attention. If I am athletically gifted, I may use my ability to receive affection and adulation from others. All of our natural gifts then become a vehicle to earn love (performance-based behaviors).

We do so many things for love—*I will please you, I will perform for you, I will rebel against you, I will run away from you, I will be really cute or nice for you, I will lead the group for you, or I will make trouble for you*—all for attention, affection, and acceptance. Yet, underneath all of our adaptive behaviors is a hungry child looking for love and using his or her innate God-given gifts to get it. But the sad reality is, as I have said many times, we do not want to be loved for what we *do*: We need to be loved just for who we *are*. No matter how many oppositional or agreeable behaviors we create, they will never give us what we most desperately seek after, which is to be loved as a precious child of God.

On the layer of our *false self*, there is a list of masks, ego structures, character armor, and defensive mechanisms that we employ in different relationships and in different social settings: rebel, protector, angry, pusher, fake, loner, nice person, performer, perfectionist, clown, victim, caretaker, sarcastic, pleaser, show-off, self-righteous, and critic. Of course, these are not the only coping mechanisms we use—there are many others. As we have seen with the five SSA celebrities, they all exhibited performance-based behaviors. If only they achieved enough, if only they won the next award, if only they found Mr. or Ms. Right, if only, if only, if only, then, *then* they would feel at peace and experience the love so desperately needed. But, again, this never works. *Earned* love is not real love. The child within seeks to experience unconditional love, and that love is not something we can earn; it is something that we only receive for who we are.

The final layer of our personality is *illnesses* and *disorders*. We know that, over time, repressed emotions and faulty thinking affect our physical bodies and emotional equilibrium. We develop further symptoms as our body and soul tries to get our attention through illnesses and disorders. Yes, these are messages from deep within attempting to bring awareness so that we may begin the process of healing.

Some of these illnesses and disorders may be: (1) sexual dysfunction, either wanting to have lots of sex, affairs, homosexual behavior, or being unable to have sex, being frigid and cold; (2) physical diseases, which may be manifesting deep physiological or psychological wounds that were internalized many years ago; (3) psychological disorders such as panic attacks, phobias, eating disorders, depression, rageaholism, stress-proneness, workaholism, fear of love, suicidal behavior, violence, obsessive-compulsive disorder, and other maladaptive psychological behaviors; and (4) addictions to alcohol, drugs, substances, sex, and/or relationships. These are all reflections of our inner *dis-ease*.

From viewing the "Layers of Our Personality," you can understand that homosexuality or SSA is simply a manifestation of many unresolved feelings and experiences. Take any and every opportunity to communicate with an SSA person, listening to their thoughts, feelings and needs. If you yourself didn't speak hurtful words, then simply ask them, "Did anyone call you derogatory names because of your same-sex attraction? What was that like for you?" Listen carefully and realize that it took years for a person to develop SSA; therefore it will take time to heal. If you view the layers of the personality like layers of an onion, it is easy to understand that we grieve as we remove yet another layer around our heart. Be there to support, listen, and comfort. If you need assistance or guidance during this process, seek counseling or coaching. Refer to the list of support organizations at the back of the book, or contact PATH (www.pathinfo.org).

Spread the truth about SSA

- No one is essentially born with SSA

- No one simply chooses to have SSA

- Change is possible

If anyone repeats a lie long enough and loud enough, over time it is believed to be fact. The homosexual movement has used this strategy, which is known as the Big Lie Theory, to proliferate the homosexual myth—*born with SSA and cannot change*. If you place a frog in boiling water, he will die; on the other hand, if you place a frog in cool water, he will happily swim around. Gradually, you begin to turn up the heat, and the frog doesn't notice. Eventually the water reaches boiling point, and the frog dies.

Over the past four decades most of us have been indoctrinated into the big lie theory of homosexuality. We have been boiled alive! The media (radio, newsprint, magazines), educational system (primary, middle, high schools, colleges and universities), mental health organizations (American Psychiatric and Psychological Associations, American Counseling Association, American Medical and Pediatric Associations), entertainment industry (television, movies, Internet), political venues, and some religious institutions, all drank the Kool-Aid. We were *desensitized* (like frogs in a constant barrage of homosexual stories in the media and movies), *jammed* (made to feel bad if we had any misgivings about homosexuality or homosexual behavior), and *converted* (Oprah and other celebrities endorse homosexual persons and their relationships, and therefore so should we).

"You can forget about trying right up front to persuade folks that homosexuality is a good thing. But if you can get them to think it's just another thing, meriting no more than just a shrug of the shoulders, then your battle for legal and social rights is virtually won" (*After the Ball*, p. 177).

Voila! Magnificent! *Fait accompli*! Wait a minute, not so fast. Time to set the record straight!

Now that you have discovered the *real* facts about SSA, it is time to let the cat out of the proverbial bag—time to come out! Come out, come out, wherever you are. Share the truth about SSA with your family members, friends, at your place of worship, in your schools, at your workplace, and everywhere in your community. Don't expect most folks to say, "Wow, I didn't know that. That's really cool!" You may hear just the opposite, "You're crazy. Everyone knows that people are born gay. There's even a gay gene they discovered. Don't you know anything?"

Healing words:

"I learned that people are heterosexually designed, and that no one is essentially born with same-sex attraction or SSA."

"In fact, changing from SSA to opposite-sex attracted is possible!"

"I know that many people have successfully come out of homosexuality and are living fulfilled heterosexual lives."

"There is no such thing as a homosexual identity, only homosexual behavior."

Revolutionary! You can be loving and truthful at the same time, and not be a "homophobe" or "anti-gay." This is "*loving in the truth.*" As I said in the introduction of this book, "Truth without love is blind. Love without truth is deadly." Wherever you go, please spread the truth about SSA with a smile on your face and love in your heart. With love, we need to share this vital and life-changing information. Thousands of men and women have changed from homosexual to heterosexual. I did it, and as a therapist, I have helped hundreds around the world fulfill their heterosexual destiny.

Wherever you go, whatever you do, set the record straight! I attended my youngest son's soccer and baseball games, and spoke with other parents while we were cheering our kids on. We got to sharing about this and that, and what we do for a living. I always tell them that I am a sexual orientation therapist, helping those who experience unwanted SSA come out of homosexuality and fulfill their heterosexual potential. "What? Really? Is that possible? I thought they're born this way." That's what almost everybody says, regardless of his or her religious background or ethnicity. "Really? I thought they're born this way."

No, folks, it's not true.

Instead, when the subject of SSA comes up, say something like this: "Did you know that no one is essentially born with same-sex attraction? There is no conclusive scientific evidence that people are born that way." Some folks will not care; others will challenge you, while still others may be curious and engage in conversation. Set the record straight! Set the record straight! Set the record straight! Use every opportunity to share the truth in love. The pen *is* mightier than the sword. Words are powerful weapons. Ideas bring change and healing to the world. *Speak up, stand up, and let the healing begin.*

Loving those with SSA the right way

> Endorsing homosexual behavior and a homosexual life may give some people what they want, but it cannot give them what they truly need.

We are the solution to this situation. By understanding that men and women who experience SSA are either seeking paternal/maternal and/or fraternal love allows us to step up to the plate and stand in the gap, embodying the love of God in a tangible way. Therefore, OSA (opposite-sex attracted) men, please bless SSA men with healthy, masculine love. The same holds true for SSA women. They are seeking maternal and sisterly love. Women, if you are attracted to the opposite sex, please bless SSA women with healthy, feminine love. There has been far too much judgment of SSA men and women. Today there is too much blind acceptance of homosexuality. *It's time to set love in order.*

For too long SSA men and women were despised simply because they experienced homosexual feelings. Now, in the name of diversity and tolerance, many are endorsing homosexual behavior, thinking they are helping to right the wrongs of centuries of unjust persecution. The healthiest position is to love all people with SSA, while at the same time helping them discover their true nature and gender identity.

As you read in the stories of transformation, these men and women were desperately seeking love, affection, and acceptance. *Sex never satisfied their needs because those feelings originated in childhood, and children do not need or want sex.* SSA is always a smoke screen for unresolved wounds from the individual's past, and legitimate needs for love yet unfulfilled. Healthy relationships with heterosexual men and women will provide the love and healing they need.

Here are three simple action-steps to help any SSA person fulfill his or her heterosexual potential:

- **Listen**: Learn how to *listen* well. Hear their stories without judgment. Let them share their truth and experience being accepted for who they are.

- **Love**: This is a person who has experienced much rejection and shame throughout his or her life. Be there for him. This is the solution to heal SSA: heterosexual men embrace SSA men, and heterosexual women embrace SSA women. *Be God with skin for them.*

- **Last**: Be the last one standing. If they are "gay" identified or seek change, they need your time, touch, and talk. Statistically most homosexual relationships do not last because both are seeking what neither one of them have. SSA men are seeking healthy paternal and fraternal love, trying to incorporate their lack of gender identity by joining with someone of the same sex. SSA women are doing the same. If homosexual relationships do last, they most often become platonic in nature. *If you continue to love your SSA friend or family member, you will be the last one standing and able to help them heal and fulfill their innate heterosexual potential.*

Listen

Communication is like air for all relationships. Without sharing and listening, relationships wither away and die. Active listening is caring for the other person, showing that you are interested in his well being. Here is a list of effective listening skills; however most imperative is that you have a heart of concern.

Effective Listening Skills:

1. *Eye contact. Look into his eyes as he shares.* This lets him know that you are actually listening and connected to his sharing. It expresses acceptance of the speaker.

2. *Joining:* Join him rather than offering advice or your opinion; see from his viewpoint. Imagine what life is like living in his shoes. You don't need answers; just "join" with him as he shares about his life.

3. *Observe his body language, tone, and words.* Research shows that more information is communicated through body language and in the tone of one's voice than through actual words. Be attentive to his posture and tone. And remember that your posture is equally important to him. Lean forward as he shares, and have an open facial expression. Do not fold your arms across your chest, as this often demonstrates emotional distancing.

4. *Be quiet and KYMS: Keep Your Mouth Shut!* You don't need to have all the answers, just listen as he shares from his heart. Bite your tongue if necessary when you completely disagree. Most of us don't need answers, we just need to be seen, heard, and accepted for who we genuinely are. Remember, be Mr. or Ms. KYMS!

5. *Reflective listening.* This is a skill to reflect back what the speaker has shared. This wonderful skill works in all relationships, with our spouses, children, boss, co-workers, and friends. Practice this skill on a regular basis. It helps you deescalate when you feel like attacking the speaker. It also enables you to see life through the other person's eyes:

    a. *Paraphrase his sharing (in small increments).* For example, you paraphrase: "You felt offended when I said, 'I don't think that people are born with same-sex attraction.'" Then say, "Is that right?" or "Did I get it right?" If you're wrong, don't worry; he'll correct you. If you left something out, he will tell you. As he continues to share, paraphrase what the speaker said every few sentences. Then say, "Is there more?" Listen, and reflect. Keep paraphrasing, and asking, "Is there more?" When he says, "No, that's it," then summarize the basic contents of all that you heard. Finally you say, "Is that essentially what you said?" or "Did I understand you correctly?" If you missed something, just repeat what speaker shared until he is finished. Next you will move on to thought empathy.

Don't put your thoughts, feelings or inflection into the communication. It's OK to 100% disagree. You just need to *join* with him and reflect what you heard. In this way, he feels understood and respected.

b. *Thought empathy*: "You make sense to me because ..." For example, "It makes sense to me that you do not agree with my belief, because you think that you were born with SSA. Is that correct?" Here you imagine how he *thinks*. You are validating his thoughts. After you finish say, "Is that right?" If it's wrong, don't worry; he'll correct you. Then paraphrase what he says and say, "Is that right?" When thought empathy has been successful, you will move on to feeling empathy.

c. *Feeling empathy*: "Given all that, I imagine that you feel ..." For example, "I imagine this makes you feel hurt, offended, and upset? Is that right?" Again, don't worry if you're wrong; he'll correct you. Then repeat what you heard, "Oh, you feel ..." Once you have attained understanding of his feelings, bravo, you did it!

When you paraphrase what he said, make sure to use the same tone as the speaker. If you use a sarcastic tone, this will invalidate everything he shared. Remember, you don't need to agree; just listen. This takes a lot of practice and patience. Keep breathing!

6. Sometimes it may be too difficult for you to use the paraphrasing skill. In this case, just say the magic words: *"Thank you, [person's name], tell me more."* Again, you want to see life from his viewpoint. Get out of the way and say, "Thank you [person's name], tell me more." You will be very surprised how grateful he is to be genuinely heard. In the process, your heart will be changed as you come to understand life through his eyes.

7. *Silence.* This is one of the greatest gifts you can give another person. Don't fill the empty moments with words, comments or questions. Just "be" with him in the silent moments. It allows him to know that you are "there" for him, and it gives him the opportunity to go deeper into his mind and heart.

8. *Don't look at your watch when someone is talking to you.* This demonstrates to the speaker that you want him to finish. If you have to look at your watch, do it when *you* are sharing.

9. *Ask gentle, non-invasive questions*: "What was that like?" "How did that make you feel?" "When did you experience that emotion before in your life?" Don't ask "why" questions, because that brings the speaker into his head. Ask open-ended questions starting with "how," "what" or "when." Of course, do not be confrontational, as this will create a barrier between the speaker and you.

Practice these skills with your spouse, relatives, friends and co-workers. Like physical exercise, it takes time to develop muscles.

Practice these listening skills when things are going well. When your SSA friend or loved one is upset, then you will be ready to effectively listen. If you would like assistance in the process of healthy communication and assisting those with SSA, please contact our office for coaching and classes.

Be aware that some SSA men or women, at times, may act like a three or four-year-old, throwing a temper tantrum, demanding that everything go his or her way—in short, exhibiting narcissistic behavior. Of course, we can all be this way from time to time. This behavior is connected to the wounded child within, basically a lack of bonding and boundaries—if the child didn't sufficiently bond with his or her parent(s), if the child was indulged and not properly disciplined, if the child was abused, if the child didn't learn how to emotionally self-regulate, these and other unresolved issues may manifest in adult tantrums.

You will need to stand firm, loving and unyielding in the presence of their immature behavior. This is time to truly demonstrate real love for the hurting child who is locked deep within the adolescent or adult. Understand they may lack the ability to emotionally *self-regulate*, and don't know how to express themselves more responsibly. Listen but do not allow him to abuse or attack you, for this will not benefit him or you. "Please do not speak to me in such a manner. It is very hurtful. What do you need right now? How are you feeling?" Then listen, reflect, and continue to hold a space for them to unfold.

A note about sharing the facts about SSA with "gay" identified men or women: *Don't!*

I hope that took you off guard! You see, their lives are constructed upon two pillars: (1) "I am born gay," and (2) "I cannot change." If you so kindly and lovingly say to this person, "You were not born with SSA and you can change." Pow! Sock in the heart! You just pulled the rug out from underneath him or her. Remember the seven stages of coming out. They went through years of confusion about their SSA, years of struggle to numb their conscience, and then, against all odds, it took years to feel comfortable living as a "gay" man or woman. Now you say, "Hey, you weren't born this way and you can change." "Well, thank you and (blank) you!"

If you wish to share these facts with a "gay" identified person, first ask yourself these questions: "Am I doing this out of love? Am I willing to be there and listen to what s/he has to say? Am I willing to get involved in this person's life? Am I willing to listen, to love, and to be the last one standing in his life?"

If the answers to these questions are, "Yes," then go for it (prepare your heart well, and seek coaching if you need assistance). If not, just give as much as you are able to this person…or ignore everything I just said, and follow your heart!

Love

Love is not only a noun, not just a feeling that we have for another. It is also a verb. It is the actions by which we express care and concern (TLC: tender loving care). Love is demonstrated by our behavior. It shows our acceptance and genuine concern for the other person's happiness. There are many actions that express our love:

1. *Spend time with him or her.* In his book, *Five Love Languages,* Dr. Gary Chapman discusses different ways in which we experience love:

   1) *Words of affirmation*: verbal compliments, words of encouragement and affection.

   2) *Quality time*: spending time together, giving her your undivided attention, quality conversations, quality activities.

   3) *Giving and receiving gifts*: giving gifts represent an expression of love, give the gift of your time, make something special for her.

   4) *Acts of service*: do something for her that she cannot do for herself, teach her a skill.

   5) *Physical touch*: healthy touch communicates care and concern (more about this shortly).

Even if you just spend a few hours per week with this SSA man or woman, it lets him or her know that you care and are thinking about them. Send emails, text messages, call her on the phone just to say "Hi" and ask how she's doing. Random acts of kindness help heal the wounded heart.

By understanding the causes of SSA in a man or woman, you are better equipped to know exactly what they need to heal their wounds and fulfill unmet love needs, i.e. close relationships with male or female mentors (restoring the parent-child wound), hanging out with heterosexual friends (restoring homo-social wounds), words of affirmation about his or her gender identity (restoring both homo-emotional and homo-social wounding), etc.

2. *Mentoring.* A key ingredient to help all SSA men and women is mentoring. Almost all same-sex attracted men and women missed this important rite of passage into manhood or womanhood through bonding rituals with their father/mother and male/female peers. Some simple ideas for male mentors are taking the guys fishing, camping, athletic games, movies, etc. or accompanying women on shopping trips, participating in their hobbies or going out for coffee. Again, as you learn about their backgrounds and understand the areas of wounding, you will know more specifically which activities will help him or her heal. If he's into the arts, join him by participating in his interests.

These essential experiences join men together, finally allowing the SSA man to feel a sense of belonging. From this inner strength and sense of internalized masculinity, and after grieving the wounds of his past with healthy male mentors, opposite-sex attractions may begin to emerge. Of course, this process takes much time...as it took years for him to develop SSA.

SSA women need to be embraced and mentored by heterosexual women. Most of them missed this important rite of passage into womanhood through bonding rituals with their mothers and female peers. Remember the heartaches of Melissa Etheridge, how she never internalized her own sense of femininity because her mother never took the time to teach her, or show her how to be a woman. We learn about our own sense of gender identity through mentoring during the formative years of childhood and adolescence. If we missed those important stages of development, still, the heart yearns for those legitimate needs to be fulfilled, no matter how old one gets. Therefore, heterosexual women, please spend time with SSA women, mentor them in the ways of women, share with them, and make them feel as though they too belong to your world.

Debora, lived a homosexual life for over 18 years (earlier, you read her story of transformation). She had several long-term partners, but eventually came out of homosexuality. Many heterosexual women in her church embraced Debora, even though she was still living with her female partner. These women surrounded her with beautiful and supportive love and wouldn't let her go. She eventually left her partner because it became more and more unsatisfying. Basically, she grew out of SSA as her true femininity was called forth into the world of women.

> Healthy bonding helps heal SSA men and women.

My father was unable to demonstrate healthy paternal love, not because he wasn't a good man, not because he didn't love me, just because he hadn't experienced it himself. What I longed for was the same thing that he himself longed for and never experienced…a warm and caring father. Philip, Peter and Russell, three wonderful, loving, heterosexual men mentored me back to life. They listened to my pain. They held me through the dark nights of my life. They were there, filling in the gaps of my past. Without their active participation in my life, I would never have healed and come out straight.

It wasn't always easy for them to hear the horrors of my life. I know I put them through their paces. But true men they were, listening, loving, and lasting in my life. Because they were willing to journey with me on this path of healing, I was able to eventually recover my true self and experience the fullness of my masculinity, becoming the powerful man I was always meant to be.

There are many similar stories from men and women who have come out of SSA and fulfilled their heterosexual potential and dreams (see many powerful stories on www.Voices-Of-Change.org).

Jeff Conrad, as described in his book, *You Don't Have to be Gay*, mentored a friend who was living an active homosexual life. Through his patience and care, eventually his friend came out straight. Story after story of loving men and women, standing side-by-side with SSA strugglers, testifies to the fact that loving in the truth will eventually set them free.

3. *Speak your truth.* SSA men and women generally feel excluded from the world of their own gender, like someone on the outside looking in. Please share about your life and your personal struggles. It's a revelation for many SSA people to realize that other men and women struggle with similar issues. Remember, SSA is not really about sex; it's about lack of successful bonding and belonging with one's own gender. The healing of SSA is helping a SSA man fit in with other men, and assisting a SSA woman to fit in with other women.

Let the SSA person know that we heterosexual men and women are just as messed up as they! The causes of all wounding are similar, just the manifestations or symptoms are different. Everyone is dealing with something, as no one had perfect parents, and we are certainly not living in a warm and supportive cultural environment...yet!

Your personal sharing is not to burden the SSA men or women, but to help them see the commonality among fellow human beings—we are all broken and in process, we all have issues.

As Goethe said, "Treat a man as he is, he will remain so. Treat a man the way he can and ought to be, and he will become as he can and should be."

Speak affirming words into his life:

"You are a strong man."

"You are very masculine."

"I admire you."

These are words that will both heal his soul and call him forth into his true masculine identify. Do the same for the SSA woman:

"You are a beautiful woman."

"You are very feminine."

"I admire you."

4. *Apologize for wrong doing or speaking if applicable.* It's OK to make mistakes. "To err is human, to forgive is divine." Let him know that you did not understand about his life and suffering before.

Healing words:

"I am truly sorry for all the thoughtless and cruel things I have spoken about you and others who experience same-sex attraction. Would you please forgive me?"

Then listen and paraphrase as you look into his eyes.

You don't need to provide answers. Just show care and concern.

5. *Say, "I love you."* Many SSA people never heard, "I love you," from their parents or good friends. This need for affirmation and acceptance most often became eroticized during and after puberty. They seek love and acceptance through sexual behavior. It never works.

> Simple words to heal the lonely and broken heart:
>
> "I love you just as you are."

Repeat these words often, calling them forth into their true gender identity. "I love you just as you are." Again, many SSA men and women never heard these words from their same-sex parent or peers.

6. *Create warm and welcoming homes and places of worship.* This is a battle of love, and whoever loves the most and the longest wins. Let me repeat this motto once again:

> *This is a battle of love, and whoever loves the most and the longest wins.*

The prize in this case is the life of a precious SSA man or woman. The homosexual community has created many organizations and places for "gay" identified men and women to hang out, to feel safe and accepted. It is our turn to turn the tide and create warm and welcoming homes and places of worship where all SSA men and women will feel comfortable, loved, and accepted.

Perhaps you read the book or saw the movie, *The Blind Side*. This is a beautiful example of a family who welcomed in a young man who had no "home," except living on the streets. This courageous act of love saved Michael Ohr's life and put him on the road to success.

- Educate your family members about the truth of SSA.
- Share this book with family and friends.
- Tell them about the stories of change.
- Visit websites that offer help and understanding about SSA (see the list of organizations at the back of the book).

- Teach your religious leaders about the facts of SSA—no one is essentially born this way, they didn't simply choose to have SSA, and change is possible. Perhaps they too were either judgmental of SSA people, or simply endorsing their behavior.

- Teach the facts with love in both your home and place of worship.

- Create a caring community, safe places for all SSA men and women to finally feel loved and accepted.

7. *Healthy touch heals*: Appropriate physical affection is an expression of caring for the other person. An arm around the shoulder, holding a hand, and a healthy hug are acts of love. Most SSA men felt excluded from the world of men while growing up, and many SSA women felt excluded from the world of women. Listening, learning from them, and caring is the greatest gift you may offer these precious, sensitive souls.

Richard and his youngest son Alfred demonstrating healthy touch.

Many of us confuse healthy touch with sex, which is unhealthy and inaccurate. We *can* physically touch without being or becoming sexually intimate. We need to learn to separate a healthy embrace from sex by displaying appropriate physical affection without any thought or desire for sexual intimacy. A strong and genuine hug allows both the giver and receiver to feel a sense of warmth, connection, and love. Practice this first with family members: stand close, look into each other's eyes, and embrace. Breathe, give and receive. Don't rush, keep breathing, giving and receiving. Healthy hugs heal and refresh our soul. Ten hugs a day keeps the doctor away!

Men and women who experience SSA are most often touch-deprived, hungering for physical affection from members of the same sex. Most did not sufficiently bond with their same-sex parent and/or same-sex peers. After going through puberty, those legitimate needs for bonding became eroticized and/or sexualized. Then the world told them, "You are gay," or "You are lesbian." *That is not true.* Their same-sex attractions represent the legitimate need of a child or pre-adolescent for healthy connection with members of the same sex, a sense of belonging, and fitting in. In fact, encouraging them to act upon their homosexual inclinations will only obstruct the fulfillment of their basic needs for belonging because those needs are that of a child.

Heterosexual men and women are the solution to this conundrum. Opposite-Sex Attracted (OSA) men, please express healthy male love and physical affection toward SSA men. OSA women please embrace SSA women. Hugging, an arm around the shoulder, walking hand in hand by two men or two women is normal in the Middle East, Asia, and other parts of the world. Unfortunately, we in the Western world have long equated touch with sex. This distortion has made many men oversexed and women undernourished. If you are able to give the gift of a healthy embrace to a SSA man or woman, you may help restore and save someone's life. Simple acts of affection—hugging, arm around the shoulder, or just being buddies with a SSA man, close to a SSA woman—this is something they may have never experienced in their lives.

> A word to the wise: Do not expect that because you are now genuinely displaying tender, loving care, they will turn around and become straight! *Once healing begins, change follows.* It took many years for this sensitive soul to develop SSA. Therefore, it will take time to heal their wounds with healthy love. Be patient and consistent.

It bears repeating: *Once healing occurs, change follows.* You don't need to worry about changing anyone else but yourself. God will do the changing, not us. Our job is to be there for this wonderful man or woman, showing unconditional love.

The homosexual community is embracing these wounded children, providing a "safe" place for them to share their heartaches and needs. *Straight and late* is how most of us have been. Let's start now, beginning to turn the tide by offering our hearts, hands, and homes to those who experience SSA, whether they choose to change or not.

Offer Love that Will Last

Statistically, homosexual relationships do not last. If they do stay together, most male partners agree to have sex outside their relationship: "The expectation for outside sexual activity was the rule for male couples and exception for heterosexuals" (David McWhirter and Andrew Mattison, *The Male Couple*, Prentice-Hall, New Jersey, 1984, p. 3). Many recent studies confirm this fact. One of Germany's leading sexologists, a self-proclaimed homosexual and university lecturer Dr. Martin Dannecker, published a study. Out of 900 male respondents living in a steady relationship, 83% (747 respondents) said they had had frequent homosexual contacts outside their steady relationships within the last 12 months (Dannecker, M: "Der homosexuelle Mann in Zeichen von Aids," Hamburg 1991, p. 103.).

In *The Sexual Organization of the City,* University of Chicago sociologist Edward Laumann argues that "typical gay city inhabitants spend most of their adult lives in 'transactional' relationships, or short-term commitments of less than six months" (Adrian Brune, "City Gays Skip Long-term Relationships: Study Says," *Washington Blade,* February 27, 2004, p. 12.).

The Dutch study of partnered homosexuals, which was published in the journal *AIDS*, found that men with a steady partner had an average of eight sexual partners per year (Maria Xiridou, et al, "The Contribution of Steady and Casual Partnerships to the Incidence of HIV Infection among Homosexual Men in Amsterdam," *AIDS* 17 (2003): 1031.)

In their study of the sexual profiles of 2,583 older homosexuals published in the *Journal of Sex Research*, Paul Van de Ven et al. found that "the modal range for number of sexual partners ever [of homosexuals] was 101-500." In addition, 10.2 percent to 15.7 percent had between 501 and 1,000 partners. A further 10.2 percent to 15.7 percent reported having had more than one thousand lifetime sexual partners" (Paul Van de Ven et al., "A Comparative Demographic and Sexual Profile of Older Homosexually Active Men," *Journal of Sex Research* 34 (1997): 354.).

When a SSA man begins to internalize the love of many OSA men, his love tank will become filled. This in turn will begin to transform his inner being, and eventually his need for homosexual relationships will naturally wane. Once again, one and one equals two. When a man finally internalizes his sense of masculinity, he will naturally be attracted to that which is different, a woman.

A fellow therapist of mine told me about a former client. This man was an active homosexual and lived with his male partner. He had no intention of coming out of homosexuality, he just wanted to deal with certain issues in his life. During the course of therapy, two heterosexual men at his work (he was the owner and boss) began to shower him with affection. They were very physical, putting their arms around him at various times, and invited him out for a drink, or just to pal around.

As these relationships deepened, and this "gay" identified man felt more accepted by the heterosexual men, he began to feel increasingly ill at ease with his partner, and asked him to move into another room in their house, as he no longer wanted a physical relationship. Over time, as the intimacy and healthy bonding occurred with his two heterosexual friends, eventually he asked his partner to leave and they broke up. Yes, his SSA gradually diminished as he too worked on unresolved issues of his past, and eventually opposite-sex attractions ensued!

Standing in the gap, as loving mentors and friends is the solution to the homosexual dilemma.

- Heterosexual men are the antidote to help SSA men heal their sense of gender identity.

- Heterosexual women are the antidote to help SSA women heal their sense of femininity.

If you disagree with homosexual behavior, do not harp on this. Judgment never works! I promise you will lose your friend or loved one to the homosexual community. Judgment never works because they are already detached and disconnected, looking for unattained love through someone of the same sex. *Win his or her heart, and the head will follow.* Remember SSA represents a legitimate need for unattained love. The world told them, "You're born gay," and that's that. We know this is *not* true, but they don't know this important fact. As they seek love through same-sex relationships, your love will stand the test of time, while most homosexual relationships are short lived. Be the last one standing, embrace with all your heart, and you will help save a life.

This is a battle of love.

Whoever loves the most and the longest wins!

Never Give Up.

Conclusion

The media, movies and television continue to mislead us, not only about the nature of homosexuality, but also about the nature of conflict resolution. The constant battles between opposing forces create a lose-lose scenario. It only perpetuates a sick system—fighting begets fighting begets fighting. It will never end. Every battle, no matter who is wrong or right, will never generate lasting change because hurting people continue to hurt people.

Martin Luther King, Jr., Mahatma Ghandi, and Nelson Mandela got it right! They knew that only through non-violent resistance, by forgiving those who wronged them, and through embracing one's seeming opposition, lasting change occurs.

Why? Because there is no "evil" per se behind harsh or unkind actions, *there is only lack of love.* Fighting among individuals and couples, within families, between neighbors, religions, races, and nations is really about the same thing: "Do I feel loved, accepted, and cared for, or do I feel rejected and unloved?"

Ignorance and lack of love are the enemy.

At the conclusion of the movie, *The Dark Crystal*, a successful resolution was fulfilled when opposing forces joined together to form a whole. Then the darkness ended and the future was bright. This is our cue how to reconcile with anyone who experiences SSA.

> *Change ensues when healing occurs.*

Many people believe they must fight *against* homosexual legislation—homosexual marriage rights, homosexual adoption rights, homosexuals in the military, homosexual education in public schools, homosexual clergy, etc. Others fight *for* homosexual persons to have additional rights. I believe that both approaches will ultimately fail. As we have seen in many European countries that fully accept, legalize and endorse homosexual behavior, many of these same-sex attracted men and women are still quite unhappy in their personal lives. Simply fighting against homosexual legislation will not solve this dilemma.

We can either be part of the problem by not taking any action, or we can participate in changing history by reaching out in love, forgiveness, and understanding.

> *The homosexual issue will NOT be solved by politics, science, media, or education. The solution is in your hands, within your heart, inside your mind, and by your actions. The sooner we get involved, the sooner the resolution occurs. It is up to you and me to reach out, listen, love, and be the last one standing.*

Here is a Formula to Resolve the Homosexual Dilemma: 1–1–1

One person or one family, love one SSA man or woman.

Love is the medicine to heal all pain.

Love one SSA person, and stand with him or her.

This will transform lives and end political conflicts.

Whether I am right or wrong regarding the causes of homosexuality is of no consequence. If I am right, and setting love in order works—men embracing SSA men, and women embracing SSA women—then those who experience same-sex attraction will naturally heal and come out straight. If I am wrong, it is still a win-win scenario, as all persons who experience SSA will finally be heard, healed, and embraced by their family and friends. The simple acts of listening, loving, and being the last one standing in the life of a SSA person will be life-changing.

As Dr. Martin Luther King commissioned, *"Darkness cannot drive out darkness; only light can do that. Hate cannot drive out hate; only love can do that."* Once again, I mentioned in the introduction to this book, *"Truth without love is blind, and love without truth is deadly."* Forgive, understand, and love with all your heart!

Many use the so-called, "love argument," promoted by homosexual activists and their followers in the media, entertainment industry, political and religious communities. It goes something like this:

"We must love all gays without trying to make them change because they are born this way. We must give them the same rights for marriage and adoption as all heterosexual couples. Let them live as they want. Stop hurting gays! God is love." (Pro-homosexual Christians say, "Jesus never said a word about homosexuality.)"

This is blind love because it denies the very fact that people are not created with SSA. Love fills the sails of the ship, but without the rudder of truth it will go astray. Having same-sex attraction is a symptom of much deeper unresolved issues. Truth without love is blind, because it does not see into the heart of men and women dealing with SSA. Love without truth is deadly, because it may lead someone into a life that will ultimately betray his or her essence. There are consequences to homosexual behavior, i.e., HIV, AIDS, higher rates of drug and alcohol addiction, high rates of suicide. Many activists will say this is because of socialized prejudice. This is partly true, but mostly these unhealthy behaviors are symptoms of the causes that led someone to experience SSA. In the Netherlands, where homosexual marriage has been legal for many years, researchers have found a higher incidence of mental illness and drug and alcohol addiction within the homosexual community than in the heterosexual community. Having all the same "rights" as heterosexuals did not resolve their internal conflicts. We need to address this crisis with love and truth in equal measure.

There *is* another side to tolerance: understanding the real facts about SSA and loving the right ways. "I love you. I know that there is a deeper truth behind your SSA. I am here for you. I love you just as you are. I will stand with you no matter what."

What if it was *you*, or your *child*, or your *parent*, or your *friend*, or your *pastor*, *priest*, *rabbi*, or *neighbor*? LGBT activists did what most people of good conscience and faith failed to do. They taught us to treat SSA men and women with dignity and respect. Most people of faith failed to do that until homosexual activists brought the issue out of the "closet." Now, in the name of tolerance, diversity, and equality, the truth has been suppressed. This is to the detriment of everyone who experiences SSA and their loved ones.

Let us work together to end the hate and hurtful comments about anyone who experiences SSA. It's time to step up to the plate and listen, love, and last. *Whoever loves the most and the longest will win.* Let us preserve the family—one man and one woman—by learning to love those who experience SSA the right way!

If you feel inspired, get involved with SSA healing ministries and organizations (see the list at the back of the book). They need to hear from people like you, so please support organizations that are doing this type of work.

...the greatest of these is love...

A chain is only as strong as its weakest link. If every church, synagogue, and mosque would launch a **Love One SSA Person Campaign**, all this political nonsense would be over.

Imagine the impact of one family mentoring one SSA person for one year, whether s/he chooses to change or not. Whatever the outcome, love is the medicine that will heal that person's pain. By demonstrating real love, by helping to heal their broken heart, we know that remarkable and lasting change will ensue.

Remember the concluding remarks of *After the Ball*: "Keep your rage, we cannot tolerate injustice." Let us help dissipate their rage. Please show all persons who experience SSA the right kinds of love to soften and win their hearts. It starts by one person loving another, by one family mentoring a SSA man or woman.

Recommended Reading

Male Homosexuality

1. *Coming Out Straight: Understanding Same-Sex Attraction*, 3rd Edition, Richard Cohen, M.A., PATH Press, Bowie, MD, 2016.

2. *Reparative Therapy of Male Homosexuality*, Joseph Nicolosi, Ph.D., Jason Aaronson Press, New York, 1991.

3. *Growth into Manhood*, Alan Medinger, WaterBrook Press (Shaw), Colorado Springs, CO, 2000.

4. *Homosexuality: A New Christian Ethic*, Elizabeth Moberly, Ph.D., Attic Press, Inc., Greenwood, SC, 1983.

5. *You Don't Have to Be Gay: Hope and Freedom for Males Struggling with Homosexuality*, Jeff Conrad, Pacific Publishing House, Newport Beach, CA, 2001.

6. *Practical Exercises for Men in Recovery of Same-Sex Attraction (SSA)*, James Phelan, Psy.D, Morris Publishing, Kearney, NE, 2006.

7. *A Young Man's Journey: Healing for Young Men with Unwanted Homosexual Feelings*, Floyd Godfrey, Create Space, 2012.

Female Homosexuality

1. *The Heart of Female Same-Sex Attraction: A Comprehensive Counseling Resource*, Janelle Hallman, InterVarsity Press, Downers Grove, IL, 2008.

2. *Restoring Sexual Identity: Hope for Women Who Struggle with Same-Sex Attraction*, Anne Paulk, Harvest House, Eugene, OR, 2003.

3. *Female Homosexuality: Choice without Volition*, Elaine V. Siegel, Ph.D., Analytic Press, Hillsdale, NJ, 1988.

4. *Practical Exercises for Women in Recovery of Same-Sex Attraction*, James Phelan, Debora Barr, Phelan Consultants, LLC, 2011.

Books for Parents, Family Members & Friends

1. *Gay Children, Straight Parents: A Plan for Family Healing*, Richard Cohen, M.A., PATH Press, Bowie, MD, Revised Edition, 2016.

2. *A Parent's Guide to Preventing Homosexuality*, Joseph Nicolosi, Ph.D. and Linda Ames Nicolosi, InterVarsity Press, Downers Grove, IL, 2002.

3. *Out from Under: The Impact of Homosexual Parenting*, Dawn Stefanowicz, Annotation Press, Enumclaw, WA, 2007.

Genetic and Biologic Theories of Homosexuality

1. *Homosexuality and the Politics of Truth*, Jeffrey Satinover, M.D., Baker Books, Grand Rapids, MI, 1996.

2. *My Genes Made Me Do It: A Scientific Look at Sexual Orientation*, Neil and Briar Whitehead, Huntington House Publishers, Lafayette, LA, 1999 (free updated edition: www.mygenes.co.nz).

General Books on Homosexuality

1. *Light in the Closet: Torah, Homosexuality and the Power to Change*, Arthur Goldberg, Los Angeles: Red Heifer Press, 2008 (second printing 2009).

2. *An Ounce of Prevention*, Don Schmierer, Word Publishing, Nashville, TN, 1998.

3. *Desires in Conflict: Answering the Struggle for Sexual Identity*, Joe Dallas, Harvest House, Eugene, OR, 1991.

Political Influence of Homosexuality in the American Psychiatric Association

1. *Homosexuality and American Psychiatry*, Ronald Bayer, Princeton University Press, Princeton, NJ, 1981.

Organizations

- American College of Pediatricians: www.factsaboutyouth.com
- Courage/Encourage (Catholic): www.couragerc.net
- German Institute for Youth and Society: www.dijg.de
- Healing Homosexuality: www.healinghomosexuality.com
- Homosexuals Anonymous (Christian): www.homosexuals-anonymous.com
- Hope for Wholeness (Christian): www.hopeforwholeness.org
- Institute for Healthy Families (Therapeutic): www.InstituteForHealthyFamilies.org
- México: www.fundaciontudecides.org
- National Association for the Research & Therapy of Homosexuality: www.narth.com
- North Star (Mormon): www.northstarlds.org
- One by One (Presbyterian): www.oneby1.org
- People Can Change: www.PeopleCanChange.com
- PFOX: Parents and Friends of Ex-Gays and Gays: www.pfox.org
- Poland: www.odwaga.oaza.pl
- Positive Approaches To Healthy Sexuality (PATH): www.pathinfo.org
- Restored Hope Network (Christian ministries): www.restoredhopenetwork.com
- Support for children of LGBT parents: www.dawnstefanowicz.org
- Testimonies of Change: www.vocies-of-change.org
- Transforming Congregation (Methodist): www.transformingcong.org
- Witness Freedom Ministries (African-American): www.witnessfortheworld.org

About the Author

Richard Cohen, M.A.

Richard Cohen, M.A., executive director of Positive Approaches To Healthy Sexuality (PATH), is a psychotherapist, educator, and author who travels throughout the world teaching on such issues as healthy sexuality, marital relations, communication skills, parenting skills, gender identity, and sexual orientation. Over the past 26 years, he has helped hundreds in therapy and thousands through healing seminars, as well as trained over 6,000 physicians, psychologists, counselors, and ministry leaders on how to assist those dealing with gender identity and sexual orientation issues. Cohen is the author of *Coming Out Straight, Gay Children Straight Parents, Straight Talk About Homosexuality,* and *Let's Talk About Sex.*

He founded the International Healing Foundation (IHF) in 1990, and co-founded Positive Approaches To Healthy Sexuality (PATH) in 2003. Cohen travels extensively throughout the United

States, Latin America, and Europe. He is a frequent guest lecturer on college and university campuses, and at therapeutic and religious conferences. Cohen is available for consultations, speaking engagements, healing seminars, counselor training programs, and family healing sessions.

Cohen holds a bachelor's degree from Boston University and a master's of arts degree in psychology from Antioch University. For three years, he worked as an HIV/AIDS educator for the American Red Cross where he authored a statewide curriculum for foster parents and child care providers with HIV infected children.

Cohen has been interviewed by newspaper, radio and television media, including appearances on 20/20, Larry King Live, The O'Reilly Factor, and Jimmy Kimmel Live. He lives in the Washington, D.C., metropolitan area with his wife of thirty-five years, while his three adult children are making their mark in the world.

Email: pathinfo@pathinfo.org

www.pathinfo.org

Additional Resources

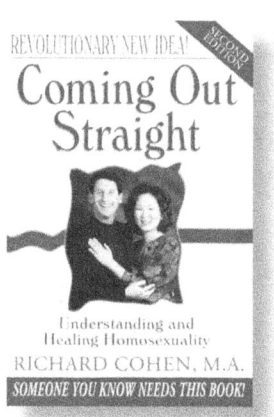

This is a landmark book that reveals a deeper understanding about the meaning behind same-sex attraction (SSA), and a successful four-stage plan for healing from homosexuality to heterosexuality. Every other chapter is a testimony of change.

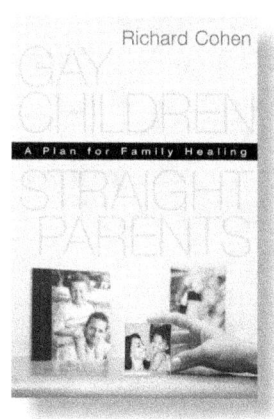

A breakthrough 12-step protocol for family and friends about helping their same-sex attracted loved ones heal and fulfill their heterosexual potential, combined with remarkable stories of transformation by parents themselves.

The 16-disc CD series and 180-page manual teaches two successful protocols: (1) helping those who experience unwanted homosexual feelings fulfill their heterosexual potential, and (2) practical interventions for their family members and friends. Therapists and ministry leaders worldwide are using our Counselor Training Program.

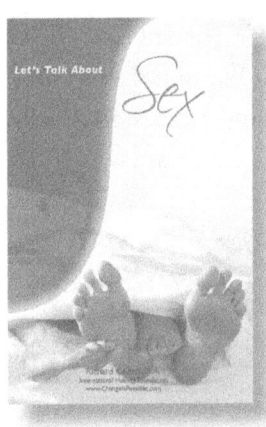

This provocative booklet gives an overview of what drives inappropriate sexual behaviors (both heterosexual and homosexual), and provides a simple four-step plan for healing.

All resources are available at: www.pathinfo.org

For more information:

Positive Approaches To Healthy Sexuality (PATH)

P.O. Box 2315

Bowie, MD 20718

Tel. 301-805-5155

Email: pathinfo@pathinfo.org

Web: www.pathinfo.org

www.ingramcontent.com/pod-product-compliance
Lightning Source LLC
Chambersburg PA
CBHW062138280526
45788CB00001B/207